Steve Th

NO NAUGHTY BITS

NICK HERN BOOKS
London
www.nickhernbooks.co.uk

A Nick Hern Book

No Naughty Bits first published in Great Britain as a paperback original in 2011 by Nick Hern Books Limited, 14 Larden Road, London W3 7ST, in association with Hampstead Theatre, London

No Naughty Bits copyright © 2011 Steve Thompson

Steve Thompson has asserted his right to be identified as the author of this work

Cover image by SWD (www.swd.uk.com)
Cover design by Ned Hoste, 2H

Typeset by Nick Hern Books, London
Printed in Great Britain by CLE Print Ltd, St Ives, Cambs PE27 3LE

A CIP catalogue record for this book is available from the British Library

ISBN   978 1 85459 205 6

CAUTION   All rights whatsoever in this play are strictly reserved. Requests to reproduce the text in whole or in part should be addressed to the publisher.

Amateur Performing Rights   Applications for performance, including readings and excerpts, in the English language throughout the world by amateurs (and by stock companies in the United States of America and Canada) should be addressed to the Performing Rights Manager, Nick Hern Books, 14 Larden Road, London W3 7ST, *tel* +44 (0)20 8749 4953,
e-mail info@nickhernbooks.demon.co.uk, except as follows:

Australia: Dominie Drama, 8 Cross Street, Brookvale 2100,
fax (2) 9938 8695, *e-mail* drama@dominie.com.au

New Zealand: Play Bureau, PO Box 420, New Plymouth,
fax (6) 753 2150, *e-mail* play.bureau.nz@xtra.co.nz

South Africa: DALRO (pty) Ltd, PO Box 31627, 2017 Braamfontein,
tel (11) 712 8000, *fax* (11) 403 9094, *e-mail* theatricals@dalro.co.za

Professional Performing Rights   Applications for performance by professionals (excluding stock companies in the United States of America and Canada, see above) in any medium and in any language throughout the world should be addressed to Independent Talent Group Ltd, 76 Oxford Street, London W1D 1BS, *tel* +44 (0)20 7636 6565, *fax* +44 (0)20 7323 0101, *e-mail* michaelmccoy@independenttalent.com

No performance of any kind may be given unless a licence has been obtained. Applications should be made before rehearsals begin. Publication of this play does not necessarily indicate its availability for amateur performance.

STEVE THOMPSON

Steve originally trained and worked as a maths teacher before turning his hand to writing. His debut play *Damages* opened at the Bush Theatre in 2004 and went on to win the Meyer Whitworth Award in 2005. In 2006, *Whipping It Up* premiered at the Bush before transferring to the New Ambassadors Theatre in the West End, and was later nominated for Best New Play in the Olivier Awards 2007. His next play, *Roaring Trade*, premiered at the Soho Theatre, London, in 2009. His television credits include *Sherlock*, *Silk* and *Doctor Who*. Steve is married to the barrister Lorna Skinner, and they live in Cambridge and Cornwall with their four children.

Other Titles in this Series

Howard Brenton
ANNE BOLEYN
BERLIN BERTIE
FAUST – PARTS ONE & TWO
    after Goethe
IN EXTREMIS
NEVER SO GOOD
PAUL
THE RAGGED TROUSERED
    PHILANTHROPISTS *after* Tressell

Jez Butterworth
JERUSALEM
JEZ BUTTERWORTH PLAYS: ONE
MOJO
THE NIGHT HERON
PARLOUR SONG
THE WINTERLING

Caryl Churchill
BLUE HEART
CHURCHILL PLAYS: THREE
CHURCHILL: SHORTS
CLOUD NINE
A DREAM PLAY *after* Strindberg
DRUNK ENOUGH TO SAY
    I LOVE YOU?
FAR AWAY
HOTEL
ICECREAM
LIGHT SHINING IN
    BUCKINGHAMSHIRE
MAD FOREST
A NUMBER
SEVEN JEWISH CHILDREN
THE SKRIKER
THIS IS A CHAIR
THYESTES *after* Seneca
TRAPS

Ariel Dorfman
DEATH AND THE MAIDEN
PURGATORIO
READER
THE RESISTANCE TRILOGY
WIDOWS

David Edgar
ALBERT SPEER
CONTINENTAL DIVIDE
EDGAR: SHORTS
THE MASTER BUILDER *after* Ibsen
PENTECOST
THE PRISONER'S DILEMMA
THE SHAPE OF THE TABLE
TESTING THE ECHO
A TIME TO KEEP
    with Stephanie Dale

Debbie Tucker Green
BORN BAD
DIRTY BUTTERFLY
RANDOM
STONING MARY
TRADE & GENERATIONS
TRUTH AND RECONCILIATION

Ayub Khan-Din
EAST IS EAST
LAST DANCE AT DUM DUM
NOTES ON FALLING LEAVES
RAFTA, RAFTA...

Liz Lochhead
BLOOD AND ICE
DRACULA *after* Stoker
EDUCATING AGNES ('The School
    for Wives') *after* Molière
GOOD THINGS
MARY QUEEN OF SCOTS GOT
    HER HEAD CHOPPED OFF
MEDEA *after* Euripides
MISERYGUTS & TARTUFFE
    after Molière
PERFECT DAYS
THEBANS

Conor McPherson
DUBLIN CAROL
McPHERSON PLAYS: ONE
McPHERSON PLAYS: TWO
PORT AUTHORITY
THE SEAFARER
SHINING CITY
THE VEIL
THE WEIR

Steve Thompson
ROARING TRADE
WHIPPING IT UP

Enda Walsh
BEDBOUND & MISTERMAN
DELIRIUM
DISCO PIGS
    & SUCKING DUBLIN
ENDA WALSH PLAYS: ONE
THE NEW ELECTRIC BALLROOM
THE SMALL THINGS
THE WALWORTH FARCE

Steve Waters
THE CONTINGENCY PLAN
FAST LABOUR
LITTLE PLATOONS
THE UNTHINKABLE
WORLD MUSIC

For my sister, who made me do the Python sketches with her

And for Alice, of course

No Naughty Bits was first performed at Hampstead Theatre, London, on 8 September 2011, with the following cast:

MICHAEL	Harry Hadden-Paton
NANCY	Charity Wakefield
TERRY	Sam Alexander
OSTERBERG	Clive Rowe
FRANKLIN	Issy van Randwyck
MYERS	Joseph May
FRIED	John Guerrasio
LASKER	Matthew Marsh

Director	Edward Hall
Designer	Francis O'Connor
Lighting Designer	Rick Fisher
Sound Designer	Matt McKenzie
Casting Directors	Suzanne Crowley and Gilly Poole

Characters

The Pythons
MICHAEL
TERRY
NANCY

The Network
MYERS
FRANKLIN

The Law
OSTERBERG
FRIED
LASKER

This play is fiction – my fantasy version of what occurred in December 1975.

Thanks to all the people who contributed along the way: Ed Hall, Tony Clark, Neil Grutchfield and Roxana Silbert. Sincere thanks to Michael Palin, Terry Gilliam and Nancy Lewis-Jones for generously sharing their time and their memories.

This text went to press before the end of rehearsals and so may differ slightly from the play as performed.

ACT ONE

Pre-show announcement.

VOICE. Good evening. The producers would like to make it
clear that the play you are about to see is a work of fiction.
(*Beat.*) Yes, it was inspired by real events. But it's still
fiction. Totally. (*Breath.*) Apart from some bits in Act Two.
The big court scene. Some of that's real. About half. Well,
not half. A bit less. But still fiction mostly. A couple of lines
are taken from the original court transcripts – but the rest of
the play is fiction, *definitely.* (*Pause.*) Michael Palin did chat
to us a bit, you know. He shared a few memories.
Reminisced over a cup of tea. And Terry Gilliam was able to
spare us half an hour when he was back from LA. We had a
drink with him in Costa up in Highgate. But some of the
protagonists are in their seventies, so you can't really expect
them to remember the incident in detail. So we had to make
it up. That's to say it's inspired by a true story. But not a true
story. Hope that's clear. Good. (*Long pause. And just when
you think the play is about to start...*) The thing is, you have
to be so careful. You want to entertain, you want to make the
evening memorable. But then you don't want to offend
anyone who was actually involved, albeit thirty-six years
ago. So – fiction fiction fiction. Let's be absolutely clear
before we get going with the show. And if anyone from
network television is here tonight: thanks for coming and we
absolutely love what you do.

1. Spotlight

Opening music: 'The Liberty Bell' march by John Philip Sousa played by a full brass band.

The music ends abruptly – the sound of a needle scratching the surface of an LP.

A spotlight comes up. MICHAEL *(thirties) stands alone. It's 1975. He wears an open-necked shirt and flared jeans.*

MICHAEL. Two TV aerials fall in love and get married. Lousy wedding. Terrific reception.

I said to my gym instructor, 'Can you teach me to do the splits?' He said, 'How flexible are you?' I said, 'I can't do Tuesdays.'

I said to my Doctor, 'Doc, I can't stop singing the "Green, Green Grass of Home".' He said, 'That sounds like Tom Jones Syndrome'. I said, 'Is that common?' He said, 'It's not unusual.'

Pause.

Absurdity, allusion, analogy, exaggeration, faulty reasoning, play on words, reproach. Freud tells us there are actually only seven types of joke.

Here's another.

Two women are watching TV, but every show is a repeat of something they've already seen. Well, they're getting more and more frustrated, so one of them presses a little button beside her – a button with an electric cable attached – and at the other end of the cable… there's this little Asian man, standing naked in a loincloth and a turban. When the woman presses the button, the current flows into him and gives him a painful shock. And the Indian changes the channel and then writhes around in pain.

Silence.

No?

I suppose it's a lot to do with how you tell it.

Scene suddenly opens out into…

2. Garden

London, winter.

MICHAEL *and* NANCY *in a suburban garden. The background noise of a residential neighbourhood.*

NANCY *is twenty-four. American; intelligent; dry. In her hands, she holds a videotape.*

MICHAEL. Me?

NANCY. Yes.

MICHAEL. Me.

NANCY. Uh-huh.

MICHAEL. No. I can't. I can't. Sorry.

NANCY. Look…

MICHAEL. I can't just drop everything and fly to New York.

NANCY *brandishes the videotape.*

NANCY. You've gotta see this. Your TV show.

MICHAEL. Thanks, I've seen it.

NANCY. Not this version. Broadcast in fifty States. You gotta take a look. (*Hands it over.*) They made some cuts. For the ad breaks.

MICHAEL. Cuts?

NANCY. Uh-huh. One laugh in four – gone.

MICHAEL (*quietly astonished*). You counted the laughs?

NANCY. It's my job.

MICHAEL. And one laugh in four…?

NANCY. Uh-huh.

MICHAEL (*gently teasing*). A quarter of the fun removed.

NANCY. I need you to fly out there and stop them cutting more.

MICHAEL. Did you ask John?

Beat. She smiles at MICHAEL *apologetically.*

NANCY. John thinks that *someone* should go.

MICHAEL. He's not prepared to go himself.

NANCY. He's…

BOTH.…in the middle of filming.

NANCY. His hotel series.

MICHAEL. I heard. (*Beat.*) Eric…?

NANCY (*quoting Eric*). 'We should just turn a blind eye.'

MICHAEL (*laughs – a little scorn*). Of course. Might tarnish his reputation in Hollywood. So… You thought I'd be an easy bet. Yeah? Pliable old Michael. Apparently I'm caretaker. Sweep the rubbish up and switch off the lights. Is that what they told you? I'm a pushover and I never say 'no' to a favour. (*Pause. Looks at her.*) I don't know you.

NANCY (*keen and eager*). I'm Nancy.

MICHAEL. I know your name.

NANCY. I work for your American management.

MICHAEL. I don't know *you*. (*Breath.*) We have 'people'. When success comes… there's lots of 'people'.

NANCY. I'm your US promoter.

MICHAEL. You count the laughs? That's an actual job. And we pay you.

NANCY. Look, we're concerned…

MICHAEL. Because twenty-five per cent of the giggles have been axed. It's 'three-quarters as funny' as it used to be. How d'you measure it? What's the industry standard here? Two sniggers makes a laugh? Five titters to the snigger, hm?

NANCY. Fly back with me.

MICHAEL (*tosses the tape back to her*). Sorry. No. No way. Can't do it.

NANCY. Look…

MICHAEL. Can't come. Not the week before Christmas. I've got commitments too. I mean, I may not be filming my own series but my diary's just as busy. This week is a total no-no. (*Pause. Has to think hard what.*) My son's play.

NANCY. What?

MICHAEL. His Christmas panto.

NANCY. Your *son*?

MICHAEL. He's a snowflake. At school. I'm afraid I have to go. (*Breath.*) My wife's done his outfit. His PE kit. Sewn with little bits of tinsel. I can't miss it, you know. I don't want him growing up bitter 'cause he was the only snowflake whose dad wasn't in the audience.

NANCY (*cautiously*). He's not playing Hamlet, though.

MICHAEL. No. But this is Gospel Oak. Half the parents in the playground work in TV. Bill Oddie's made his daughter a whole outfit. Bill will be there, cheering. So must I be.

Pause. He's smiling. She isn't. She's clearly a little anxious.

NANCY. My boss expects me…

MICHAEL. Of course. Yes. I understand.

NANCY. I have to get this thing sorted.

MICHAEL. So you came to me? 'Mike's your guy – he's got nothing in the pipeline. Career in tatters. If you need something doing – he'll be free.' (*Pause.*) I wanted to go on, did they tell you that? To make more series.

NANCY. Yes.

MICHAEL. It wasn't my decision to end it. (*Breath.*) John...

NANCY. Yes.

MICHAEL. *He* was the one who pulled the plug. He's not in
the last series. They wouldn't let us carry on without him.
(*Breath.*) One minute I'm standing there; I'm in the welly
boots and knotted hanky; comic royalty. Next thing you
know – John says he's bored. And we're all bundled out the
back door of the BBC.

NANCY. Look, I've been asked to...

MICHAEL. Can't roll up to the Labour Exchange and ask if
they've any jobs going in 'light entertainment'. My only
professional experience is dressing up in false tits. How
d'you rate my prospects?

NANCY. Look, I...

MICHAEL. Aside from slapping people with fish, I've had no
proper jobs since university. Someone else can fly to New
York. I've got to stay here and hunt for a new career. Sorry.

Silence.

NANCY *fumbling around for something to say.*

NANCY. Groups sometimes lose their lead singer.

MICHAEL. I beg your pardon?

NANCY. Peter Gabriel left Genesis.

MICHAEL (*no idea*). Did he?

NANCY. Last year. They made a really good album without
him. The drummer sang.

He looks at her – bewildered.

I work with rock bands too.

MICHAEL (*smiles*). I'd stick to that in future, probably.

NANCY. Listen – a major TV franchise has picked up your
final series. First time on network TV. You can still make it
big in the States.

MICHAEL. 'Big'. We don't exist any more.

NANCY. America doesn't realise!

He looks at her, fascinated for the first time.

You're becoming a cult, did you know that? People swapping LPs; watching it late-night; college rooms. Kids sneaking down at midnight. Tuning in whilst parents are asleep. You're on the verge of something huge. They made the series into two big TV specials. Three episodes in each one. Ninety minutes. (*Breath.*) This was the first.

MICHAEL. So there's another?

NANCY. Yes. One more chance. One chance to break the US. (*Wielding the tape.*) This is your new career I'm holding here! (*Digs into her handbag and produces a plane ticket.*) It doesn't matter... doesn't matter that John has cut loose. The whole of America is just waking up to you. Somebody needs to fly over and make sure your network debut is as goddamned funny as possible!

Beat. MICHAEL *takes the ticket. Sees two other tickets in the bundle.*

MICHAEL. There's three tickets.

NANCY. Uh-huh.

MICHAEL. Who is the other one for? (*Numbering on his fingers.*) John and Eric turned you down. Jonesy's out of the country. Graham...

NANCY. Not an option.

MICHAEL. No. (*With slight trepidation.*) So that leaves...

NANCY. Yes.

MICHAEL. The Yank.

NANCY. He's keen to come.

MICHAEL (*deep sigh*). He's keen to pick a fight, you mean. (*Breath.*) He fucking hates his countrymen.

Scene fades.

The noise of an English garden blends into the sound of an aircraft taking off.

3. Airport

Touchdown in New York. JFK.

Two men burst through the barrier at airport arrivals.

TERRY GILLIAM: *a long-haired artist in a loud shirt, Afghan coat and glasses. He's wheeling his luggage on a little trolley.*

MICHAEL*'s trolley is empty – still waiting for his luggage to come off the carousel.*

TERRY. Ten years!

MICHAEL. Oh Lord!

TERRY. Ten long years.

MICHAEL. How's it feel? You going to kiss the ground?

TERRY. I'm gonna piss on it! Goddamned fucking country.

MICHAEL. Well, it's good to see you've put it all behind you, Terrence.

TERRY (*bellowing to anyone who will listen*). I curse you all, America – for what you made me do to Marty Feldman!!

MICHAEL. Oh, goody. Here we go!

TERRY. First cartoon I ever did! Marty's US show.

MICHAEL. The Rubens nude.

TERRY (*not listening to* MICHAEL). The Rubens nude. They fucking censored it!

MICHAEL. Cut two circles out.

TERRY. Cut two circles out to hide her tits. (*Holding two imaginary breasts on himself.*)

MICHAEL. Really?

TERRY. Fucking arseholes.

MICHAEL. Bad luck. And what about her vagina?

TERRY. A piece of pie!

MICHAEL. No!

TERRY. To hide her vagina!

MICHAEL. Really?

TERRY (*shakes his head*). Peter Paul Rubens! Master of the Flemish Baroque. The guy survives religious persecution in *his* lifetime. Can't get past the network censors in sixties' America. I tell you – only TV has the goddamned arrogance to meddle with a seventeenth-century masterpiece. If Jesus came back now and went on TV, there'd be some guy asking: 'These commandments, pal… You absolutely sure you need ten of them?'

MICHAEL. Mm.

TERRY. I tell you, Mike – not this time. NOT THIS TIME! This time these sanctimonious bastards are not going to touch me.

TERRY empties his pockets of sweet wrappers and crisp bags. He starts to screw them up and throw them at the airport staff.

MICHAEL. Yep. I'm not sure that the airport staff at JFK are personally responsible for TV-editing policy.

TERRY. Our show is a symbol.

MICHAEL. Of?

TERRY. Intellectual freedom. This isn't a business trip, Mike. It's a fucking crusade. One joke in four – gone! – so they can sell the audience peanut butter. I'm going to this meeting packing a .38, a blowtorch and a halberd.

MICHAEL trying to wrestle him away from a potential fight with everyone in the airport.

NANCY appears with a shopping bag.

NANCY. Hiya. No news about your luggage. Sorry.

MICHAEL. Ah. Okay.

NANCY. TWA. Know what that stands for?

ALL. 'Try Walking Across'.

NANCY. Worse than useless. Anyway, I bought you some stuff. (*Hands him the bag.*) Oh. I've got something here that'll cheer you up.

Beat. She roots around in her bag and then hands him a copy of New Yorker *magazine. Points to a story.*

'Stars fly in to take on the network.'

MICHAEL (*reads – incredulous*). How did they get hold of this?

NANCY (*delighted with herself*). I gave Herzberg an interview. Yesterday. (*Delighted.*) Landmark case.

MICHAEL. What?

TERRY. Hell, yeah.

NANCY. David and Goliath. (*Reads over his shoulder.*) 'The only writers in history who've done battle with a network.'

MICHAEL (*bemused*). I don't understand. Why get the press involved? We want them to show the next programme the way we made it. Don't you think we might lose their goodwill when they read this?

NANCY (*shrugs*). Hey. Free publicity.

MICHAEL. Publicity – yep. But there's a price for it. (*Slams the paper back in her hands.*) 'Rock promotion.'

NANCY. Look...

MICHAEL. That's your background. 'Rock promotion.'

NANCY. Sure.

MICHAEL. Getting people to chuck stuff out of hotel rooms. Get us noticed. And *you* get noticed.

NANCY. If it works...

MICHAEL. Shout. Shout loud. That's your method here.

NANCY. It's just the way we do it.

MICHAEL. Great. So I've got Terry trying to wreak his revenge on the nation that spurned him by messing up his very first painting. And I've got you trying to stir up a media frenzy. Everything bodes well for a really constructive meeting.

NANCY. Car's waiting.

Scene fades.

4. Hotel room

Evening.

MICHAEL *is in his hotel room. He lies on the bed, speaking softly into the telephone.*

MICHAEL (*on telephone*). It's my job. (*Breath.*) I know it's hard. (*Beat.*) Yes, the TV show. (*Breath.*) Yes. The one where Daddy wears the hanky. (*Beat.*) I need to make sure it's… good. (*Breath.*) Yes, that's right, but then sometimes people want to change it. (*Breath.*) Well, that's difficult, poppet. It's like when Willy put that paint on Womble. And you didn't want him to. (*Breath.*) What about you?

A knock at the door. NANCY *enters.*

(*Listens.*) Wow. Fantastic. That big?

NANCY *taps her watch.*

Er… Look, I've got to go. Yep. (*Listens.*) Bye. Love to Mummy. Bye now.

And he hangs up.

NANCY. Good news?

MICHAEL. Mm?

NANCY. What was 'fantastic'? (*Breath.*) Something was 'fantastic'.

MICHAEL (*remembering*). Yes. He did a very long wee. A minute long.

NANCY. And he times it for you?

MICHAEL. He thinks I'm interested.

NANCY. In the duration?

MICHAEL. Apparently. (*Breath*.) We call it my 'naughty business'.

NANCY. Sorry?

MICHAEL. It's the way he understands it. 'My daddy's in the naughty business.'

NANCY. Ah.

MICHAEL. I do jokes about wee-wees and bums. So that's what we talk about.

NANCY. Same as most men, in fact.

Another knock at the door. TERRY *enters. He's carrying a suit bag with the logo of a fancy dress-hire shop.*

All set then?

TERRY. Yeah.

MICHAEL. Do we really have to do this?

NANCY. Look…

MICHAEL. We really have to bring in a whole big legal team? I thought the three of us would all go up to ABC, shake hands politely and, you know… just settle this like gentlemen.

TERRY. Sure. And then we could all stand round the piano and sing songs from Broadway.

MICHAEL. Why do we need to take a lawyer along?

NANCY. This won't be like the BBC.

TERRY. No. Right. These guys may be sober.

NANCY. Just meet with him, will you?

She opens the door.

Robert, hiya.

OSTERBERG *enters.*

OSTERBERG *is a smart lawyer – small and broad, rather like an armoured car. His appearance is immaculate – a suit and tie – and he carries a leather briefcase.*

Guys. This is Robert Osterberg. He's been hired by your New York legal team.

OSTERBERG *goes over to shake their hands. He is dry and oddly humourless.*

OSTERBERG (*to* MICHAEL, *as he shakes his hand*). Arthur Pewtey?

MICHAEL (*smiles, polite*). You watch?

OSTERBERG. Every show.

MICHAEL. Oh. Great.

OSTERBERG (*unappreciative*). Took me two days. Started Monday. Finished yesterday.

MICHAEL. Ah.

OSTERBERG. And you also do 'Nudge Nudge'?

MICHAEL. No. That's Eric Idle. People confuse us. (*A sideways look to* NANCY.) Basically because we're not John Cleese.

OSTERBERG (*shaking hands with* TERRY). You two fly in this morning?

TERRY. Uh-huh.

OSTERBERG. What kept you?

TERRY. Sorry?

NANCY. Fog.

OSTERBERG. Fog?

MICHAEL. Yes. Bad fog.

OSTERBERG. Really? For ten weeks? (*Breath.*)

MICHAEL. Er...

OSTERBERG. Seventy-five days of fog. That's kind of a record, isn't it? Even for Britain.

No one knows what OSTERBERG *means. Everyone turns to one another, confused.* OSTERBERG *ignores them. He opens his briefcase and takes out a file.*

TERRY. The fog was just last night.

OSTERBERG. What kept you the rest of the time, huh? Seventy-five days since they showed it. Have you just come out of hospital?

MICHAEL. What?

OSTERBERG. You guys maybe break a leg?

MICHAEL. What!?

OSTERBERG. Been consigned to a wheelchair? Stopped you boarding a plane.

NANCY. Look…

OSTERBERG. Must have been a cruel trick of fate: six of you with injuries – all unable to fly.

NANCY. Robert…

MICHAEL. We only just saw the tape.

OSTERBERG. Did you ask to see it earlier?

No one can think what to say. MICHAEL *eventually jumps in.*

MICHAEL. We… We took our eye off the ball. (*Breath.*) It's a cricketing metaphor.

OSTERBERG. Is it? (*Breath.*) You let a major TV network broadcast your show – and never asked to see an edit.

MICHAEL. No.

OSTERBERG. So, it's a metaphor for being a dumb-arse.

TERRY. I guess we're done with 'Hello'.

Pause. OSTERBERG *settles himself in a chair.*

OSTERBERG. Tomorrow we will ride the elevator to the twenty-first floor of the network tower in New York. We'll be ushered in to meet Howard Myers: the Head of Comedy. The man who put your show into ten million homes.

MICHAEL. Yes. Look...

OSTERBERG. He's got another slot for you Monday. A late-night slot. And he's gonna want to know: if it's so damned important you re-edit, why did you wait two months to knock on his door?

Beat. OSTERBERG *looks at them all. They are struggling to answer.*

How do you plan to persuade him? Or... did you think he'd just smile and restore the missing video?

TERRY. I was thinking, maybe, pillory... thumbscrews.

OSTERBERG (*poker face, to* TERRY). You're the funny one, Terry. I can tell. Gonna be a blast working for you.

MICHAEL *picks up the videotape and offers it to* OSTERBERG.

MICHAEL. It's no longer as funny.

OSTERBERG. I'm sorry?

MICHAEL. This tape.

OSTERBERG. And? (*Breath.*) And? (*Breath.*)

Still no response.

That's what you're taking to the meeting?

TERRY. It's supposed to be a comedy programme. The fact that it's not as funny, it does seem kinda relevant really...

OSTERBERG *reaches into his briefcase for a single sheet of A4. He reads the contents to them.*

OSTERBERG. Fifty-six thousand dollars.

MICHAEL. What?

OSTERBERG. He paid. For your show.

TERRY. Doesn't give him the right to butcher it.

NANCY *pats* TERRY *on the arm to restrain another imminent outburst.*

OSTERBERG. As opposed to *eighty* thousand in advertising revenue, made from those missing minutes. (*Leans back in the chair.*) Advertising isn't some sideline – filling dead air. It pays for his Florida home.

MICHAEL. But surely…

OSTERBERG. The only way he'll give you what you want is if there's some *financial penalty* involved.

Pause. The words gradually sink in.

TERRY. 'Penalty'?

OSTERBERG. We squeeze him.

TERRY. 'Squeeze'?

OSTERBERG. Yes. We sit in a room with him, grab him by the throat and squeeze hard.

Beat. The word just sits there for a moment.

NANCY. How?

OSTERBERG. The Lanham Act.

NANCY (*at sea*). Never heard of it. Sorry.

OSTERBERG. Congressman Fritz G. Lanham of the State of Texas. (*Breath.*) In this great country of ours, I can't just dig a hole in my backyard, fill it with water and put a sign up saying 'Come and enjoy a day at the Grand Canyon.' It's against the law. You can't make pale imitations. Lanham Act says so. That's what we're dealing with here. Just in case you're actually interested in persuading him.

Beat. The wheels turn.

TERRY. He can't use the name of our show?

OSTERBERG *nods.*

Not if it isn't funny?

OSTERBERG. He'd be fined. He'd be fined for putting your show on and calling it by the same name.

TERRY. 'Imitating'?

OSTERBERG. Mm. (*Beat.*) That's one possible squeeze.

TERRY. There are more?

OSTERBERG. There are three. Three ways to squeeze. We could threaten to sue for reputation.

MICHAEL. 'Sue'?

OSTERBERG. If people tune in and they think that the jokes are pretty feeble. It'll tarnish your reputation?

MICHAEL. Sorry? Did you say 'sue'?

OSTERBERG. And then we can sue for copyright. You have a contract with the BBC. Maybe do a cocktail… (*Numbering on his fingers, slowly and with emphasis.*) Reputation – copyright – Lanham. (*Beat.*) Still, if you don't need me, I'm happy to take my backside out of here. You can just tell Myers it's not funny. Cross your fingers he's a sympathetic ear.

Stands. Pause. He's waiting to see what they will do.

TERRY. How much? (*Beat.*) If you threatened to sue?

MICHAEL (*seeking to interrupt*). Er…

OSTERBERG. More.

TERRY. More?

OSTERBERG. More.

MICHAEL. 'Sue'?

OSTERBERG. More than eighty thousand in advertising. That's how we do it over here – that's America. You simply put a price tag on everything.

OSTERBERG *reaches into his case again and produces a bound A4 document. He offers it to* NANCY.

Sent over by courier.

NANCY *opens it.* MICHAEL *peers over her shoulder.*

MICHAEL. What?

OSTERBERG. The second special. The one that's going out Monday. I asked for a detailed breakdown of everything they've changed. Every little cut.

NANCY. There's masses of it!

OSTERBERG. Thirty-two. They've made thirty-two changes.

MICHAEL (*reads*). The Victorias! No way!

NANCY. What?

MICHAEL. The dancing Queen Victoria chorus line. I spent a bloody agonising day in a wig and a corset.

OSTERBERG. I don't imagine they knew that.

TERRY (*reads*). Not the Indian slave!

NANCY. What?

TERRY. Gone! Shocking the Indian slave with electrodes on his nipples.

MICHAEL. And the war film. Bollocks! I loved that.

TERRY. The phoney film announcer?

MICHAEL (*in a film announcer's voice*). 'Coming to this cinema... bisexuals!'

OSTERBERG (*listing them all*). The phoney film announcer; the Indian slave with electrodes on his nipples; and the dancing Queen Victoria chorus. We put our hands on his throat and we get 'em all back.

Silence.

MICHAEL. You said 'sue'.

OSTERBERG. I said 'threaten to sue'. (*Breath.*)

NANCY (*still at sea*). How's this work?

OSTERBERG. Well, it's Federal.

MICHAEL. I'm sorry. What... what do you mean?

OSTERBERG. We threaten him with Federal court. We tell him the time and place and the Judge's name.

OSTERBERG *reaches into his bag and produces a piece of paper.*

I've issued an injunction.

NANCY (*caught out by this*). Already?

OSTERBERG. This second show is Monday night. No time to fool around. (*Reads the page*.) The Judge rules on Friday morning. Myers has got till then. Trust me – he'll back down.

Pause.

MICHAEL. Hang on, we're not seriously... We're not seriously thinking of going to court here.

OSTERBERG. Mr Palin...

MICHAEL. That's not why I got on a plane! That's not why I came. I thought this was just a conversation...

OSTERBERG. It's the way...

MICHAEL. I thought Terry, me and Myers would sit around and barter. Maybe even have a cup of tea. Now suddenly there are lawyers in the room. And a Judge booked for Friday.

OSTERBERG. It's never gonna get that far. Believe me.

MICHAEL (*to* NANCY). I'm way out of my zone here, sorry – three thousand miles from Gospel Oak, no suitcase, and now you want me to go in to ABC and shout the word 'injunction'?

NANCY. I want you to have a career.

He opens his mouth to object.

I know it ain't your style. You're the guy who doesn't even complain when his suitcase goes missing. But just for one day – stop being the nice British guy. (*Looks at* OSTERBERG.)

OSTERBERG. Walk into ABC and pick a fight. Can you do that?

OSTERBERG *looks at* MICHAEL. MICHAEL *looks at* TERRY.

Scene fades.

We hear the Monty Python *theme music – the march – from the end of the show. It is played through the speaker system of a television*.

5. Office

The lights come up on a large conference room.

The room is dominated by a long wooden table.

At one end of the table is perched a television set, playing an episode of Monty Python's Flying Circus. (*We cannot see the screen.*)

The music to accompany the credits is coming to an end. Everyone around the table has been watching avidly: NANCY, MICHAEL, TERRY *and* OSTERBERG. *The light from the television flickers in their faces.*

OSTERBERG *has opened up his case and has taken out the videotape of the first show – now perched on the table in front of him.*

Everyone has a copy of the bound A4 document – the complete list of the cuts made to this second show. TERRY *has a pencil and he is furiously scribbling on the pages.*

He has come dressed as an English soldier from the American War of Independence.

With them is LEE FRANKLIN *– a pale-faced woman dressed in a smart suit and bold make-up. She stands up and turns off the television as soon as the theme music dies away. She takes the tape from the machine and puts it in the middle of the table.*

Now there are two tapes up for discussion – episodes one and two – laying there side by side.

FRANKLIN *turns to the company and smiles serenely – a glorious, calming smile like a religious icon from a Medieval painting.*

OSTERBERG (*blunt, emotionless*). That's it?

FRANKLIN (*still serene*). Yes.

OSTERBERG. That's what you're showing?

FRANKLIN. Yes.

OSTERBERG. That's the second special? That's the edit?

FRANKLIN. Indeed. Yes. (*Beat.*) We thought if you saw it – it might… soothe you.

OSTERBERG. Ah. Right.

FRANKLIN. It might not be as 'brutal' as you'd feared. (*A wide smile. Beat.*)

OSTERBERG *turns to* TERRY *and* MICHAEL.

OSTERBERG. Guys? How are we doing with the 'soothing'?

FRANKLIN. We're keen for your thoughts.

OSTERBERG (*to* TERRY *and* MICHAEL). They want us smiling by close of play.

FRANKLIN. Let's just say…

OSTERBERG.…no one in this building wants to see the screen go blank on Monday.

Pause. FRANKLIN *maintains her smile.* OSTERBERG *turns to his clients.*

Fellas?

TERRY *slams down his pencil. He has finished scribbling.*

He looks up – fire in his eyes. Gets to his feet – like a politician addressing his peers.

TERRY. I do have one question…

FRANKLIN. Yes?

TERRY.…this may seem strange, it's about – well – continuity.

FRANKLIN. Please.

TERRY (*pointing to the new tape*). In this new show, the one about to air, there's a sketch… a posh family, all sitting in their lounge…

OSTERBERG (*checks his document*). Discussing words.

TERRY. Yep.

OSTERBERG. Words that have a nice sound. A 'woody' sound.

FRANKLIN *searches through her bundle.*

FRANKLIN. Just let me find it.

OSTERBERG (*reading*). 'Seemly.' 'Prodding.'

FRANKLIN (*can't find it*). Er... okay...

OSTERBERG. Words that give them confidence.

TERRY. That's the one.

OSTERBERG (*reading the manuscript*). 'Sausage.' 'Foal.' 'Recidivist.'

FRANKLIN (*finally finds the page*). Yes. Here we are.

TERRY. You've made a cut in it.

OSTERBERG. Three seconds.

FRANKLIN. Have we?

OSTERBERG. So it says here. In your document. Three seconds gone.

TERRY. Okay, but what I don't understand, Miss Franklin, is why you've cut those three seconds out from the middle. (*Beat.*) The actor, my colleague there, Graham, he's playing a scene where he gets all fired up about *words*... he gets excited, starts jumping about and his wife, Eric Idle, she throws a bucket of water on him.

FRANKLIN (*checking the document*). That's what we've cut.

TERRY. Uh-huh, that's what you've cut. You've cut the water being thrown... you've cut the bucket.

FRANKLIN. Right. (*Breath.*) So...?

TERRY. So when you *cut back*, Graham is wet. When the previous second...

FRANKLIN....he was dry. I see the issue.

TERRY (*picking up the tape*). One moment totally dry, split second later the camera cuts to him he's soaked. (*Breath.*) The bucket of water, we must see it.

FRANKLIN. You're concerned about the logic.

TERRY. I'm concerned that it looks fucking terrible.

He grabs the videotape and bites it ferociously, growling like a dog with a bone. The tape spools out.

He bites a piece, chews it (tape spilling from his mouth), and spits it on the floor.

Silence.

FRANKLIN *never lets her smile fade.*

TERRY *lobs the broken videotape at her feet as a finale to the act.*

When he speaks again it is with charm and poise.

You think maybe you could explain – maybe throw some illumination on your methods? (*Breath.*)

FRANKLIN (*deadpan*). It's zany.

TERRY. What?

FRANKLIN. Zany. Your... humour. There's no logic at all. (*With a half-laugh.*) Getting excited about the word 'croquet'.

TERRY *clicks and holds up his finger as if she has just made a key point.*

TERRY. Not just 'excited', no no...

FRANKLIN. What?

TERRY. ...he's 'sexually excited'...

FRANKLIN. Well...

TERRY. ...he has a big hard-on...

FRANKLIN. I suppose.

TERRY. ...you want to amputate a quarter of the show and you've pulled out the three seconds here when Graham's got a boner.

She opens her mouth – seeking to move the conversation on.

In the montage sequence of war: where's the naked guy playing the piano?

FRANKLIN (*reads*). Yes. I see that's gone…

TERRY. Later on you've lost fourteen seconds… (*Reads.*) 'Man dressed as doorman, fumbling under skirts of woman.'

FRANKLIN. Look…

TERRY. A guy with an erection – removed; a naked guy at a piano – he's gone too… so, no boners, no bums, no masturbation. I dunno, is it me, or are we seeing some sort of broad theme?

Beat. No response.

I've put them into groups – thirty-two cuts.

He tears some pages from the document.

He has drawn giant slogans on the back of each page – big cartoon lettering with pictures attached.

He starts to pin his artwork up on the walls – brilliant Gilliam cartoon illustrations.

Sexual humour… (*Bang – he pins up a page with the word 'Sex' written on it and a helpful cartoon of someone's hand masturbating a penis.*)

Gags involving… some sort of violence… (*Bang – another that says 'Violence'. A cartoon gun to the head.*)

References to excrement… (*Bang – 'Poo-poo'. A cartoon turd.*)

References to minorities… (*Bang – 'Minorities'. A cartoon Indian slave boy.*)

Plain miscellaneous swearing. (*Bang – on the last page he has written dozens of swear words. 'Fuck', 'Bollocks', 'Wanker', 'Cunt', etc.… The page is crammed with them.*)

He points at each page like a teacher in front of a class.

Sex; violence; shit; minorities; swearing. Doesn't seem all that random really, does it? Everything – everything that's taken out from Special Number Two falls into one of those categories. (*Throws his pen down on the table.*) You're not making space for the ads…

FRANKLIN. Well...

TERRY....not any more...

FRANKLIN. We...

TERRY....it's just an excuse to gag us. You're using this to launch your own moral agenda.

FRANKLIN. That's just your interpretation.

OSTERBERG *senses they are on the ropes – seizes his moment.*

OSTERBERG. Let's look at the facts. (*Opens the script.*) What about the Montgolfier brothers?

FRANKLIN (*reading notes*). Where?

OSTERBERG. First show.

FRANKLIN *dives into a separate pile of paper and reads down a list of sketches.*

FRANKLIN. Oh, yes.

OSTERBERG (*taps his page*). 'Golden age of ballooning.' (*Reads.*) 'So on June 7th 1783, the Montgolfier brothers had a really good wash. Starting with his face and arms, Joseph Michael Montgolfier went on to wash his torso, his legs and his... er, naughty bits.' (*Pause. Looks at her.*) You bleeped it.

FRANKLIN. Mm.

OSTERBERG. You bleeped the words 'naughty bits'.

FRANKLIN. Well.

TERRY. You bleeped the punchline. The joke is no longer funny.

OSTERBERG. What's a bleep? (*Breath.*) What does it signify?

Beat. She has no answer.

It doesn't buy you time. It doesn't free up space. What's it doing?

FRANKLIN *is clearly caught out here. She sits there, silent, tight-lipped. And then...*

FRANKLIN. Certain things we're not allowed to put on air.

TERRY. 'Allowed'?

OSTERBERG. You can't say 'naughty bits'?

FRANKLIN (*shrugs*). Sorry. Refers to the genitals. (*Takes out a very thick book.*) We have a Standards and Practices Charter. Genitals are not permitted. Under any circumstances. (*Breath.*) People in Idaho will watch this.

TERRY. They don't have genitals in Idaho?

FRANKLIN. What they have is a strict moral code. This is a network. We broadcast to a nation. Not a few East Coast intellectuals.

OSTERBERG. Miss Franklin...

FRANKLIN. This isn't England. There is no 'national humour'. There are fifty States with different... (*Taps the book.*) requirements. Different tastes.

TERRY. You're trying to please 'all the people all of the time'. So you make the thing as insipid as you can. 'No naughty bits.'

NANCY. But 'Naughty bits' is gentle; it's suggestive.

OSTERBERG. 'Naughty bits' is actually there to bleep out the word 'cock'!

FRANKLIN. Look...

OSTERBERG. If you obscure it with a bleep – people are gonna think something worse was there before.

FRANKLIN. I think...

OSTERBERG. 'Dick.' Could have said the word 'dick'.

FRANKLIN. No...

TERRY. 'Bacon bazooka.'

OSTERBERG (*liking* TERRY*'s suggestion*). Nice.

FRANKLIN. We thought that...

OSTERBERG. You're forcing them to blush, you're gesturing at someone's groin and saying 'For God's sakes, don't anyone look at this filth I'm pointing at!'

FRANKLIN. Mr Osterberg...

OSTERBERG. The 'bleep' is what makes it obscene. It's the effort to conceal a thing that makes it vulgar. What's the point of trawling through the tape with a monster pair of scissors? All you do is make people curious!

FRANKLIN. I...

TERRY. Vagina!

Beat. They all turn to look at him.

Vaginavaginavaginavaginavagina. I say the word one time and you blush. I say it twenty times – I say it a hundred times and suddenly it's powerless. Say it with me.

FRANKLIN. Can we just get back...?

TERRY. Sing it with me. Sing the word 'vagina'. (*Operatic.*) 'Vagina.' To the tune of 'The Star-Spangled Banner'.

FRANKLIN. Can we not...?

TERRY (*sings*). 'Oh say can you see, by the dawn's early light, what so proudly we hailed. A big vagina...'

FRANKLIN. Mr Gilliam! (*Regaining charm and tact.*) I realise that you... you began your careers with a totally different... audience. Frat humour.

TERRY. 'Frat'?

FRANKLIN. Student.

TERRY. Of course. Yes.

FRANKLIN. The cabaret circuit. Late-night – college campuses. People pay for a ticket to the cabaret – they walk through the door – they 'invest' in the experience.

TERRY. Well then...

FRANKLIN. The television is in your home. It's sitting there just beside the sofa. A valued friend. You don't expect it to start swearing at you…

TERRY. No?

FRANKLIN. Start yelling filth; flaunting itself like a child. We are talking about a pipeline that runs into every single home – not a club for radicals.

TERRY. And you think…?

FRANKLIN. You can't use it as your mouthpiece. Not without a vigorous edit of some kind!

TERRY (*sweetly, pulls open the top of his trousers*). Perhaps you'd care to reach into here and edit this vigorously.

OSTERBERG. We're not 'soothed' yet, I'm guessing.

FRANKLIN (*still composed and charming*). Excuse me, please.

She exits.

Quickly, OSTERBERG *gathers them into a conspiratorial huddle. He holds up the list of cuts. Some of them he has circled in red.*

OSTERBERG. We still agreed on these six?

MICHAEL. Yep. That's what we said.

NANCY. Six is our minimum requirement.

OSTERBERG. These six go back and it's funny?

MICHAEL. Not 'funny'. Just…

OSTERBERG. Funny enough? Okay . Remind me, will you? (*Reading with no trace of humour whatsoever.*) I've got 'Secret love of bisexuals'.

He looks momentarily confused. MICHAEL *explains.*

MICHAEL. The war film where the pilot is in love with the navigator.

OSTERBERG (*nods*). I've got 'Dousing the erection'? Yes? (*And then realises what this is.*) Terry – that's your one where the bucket of water's been cut. (*Reads*.) Michael, your one: 'Special gaiters'…

NANCY (*carrying on*). 'Legs up on the mantelpiece.'

OSTERBERG. 'Legs up on the mantelpiece.' What's that?

MICHAEL. The one where Hamlet is discussing…

OSTERBERG.…the way to make out with Ophelia. Okay. Yep. Got that. (*Reads again*.) Got 'The chorus line of dancing Queen Victorias.' What am I missing? (*Beat. Numbering again*.) Bisexuals, hard-on, gaiters, mantelpiece.

NANCY. The dancing Queens.

OSTERBERG. Uh-huh. The dancing Queens. What else?

Beat. Everyone thinks hard.

MICHAEL (*suddenly remembers*). Shocking the Indian slave boy's nipples.

OSTERBERG (*overlapping*). Shocking the Indian slave boy's nipples! (*Makes a note*.) They have to agree to those six – or we're doing the thing. We're doing the special signal. (*They nod cautiously*.)

MICHAEL (*downbeat*). I think we should employ Bob.

TERRY (*nods agreement*). A natural.

MICHAEL. The way you read our stuff, Bob. Truly hilarious.

OSTERBERG. Thank you.

Silence.

NANCY. I can't remember. What we agreed.

MICHAEL. It was this. (*Tickles the tip of his nose with his forefinger*.)

OSTERBERG. Other hand.

NANCY. And who's doing it?

OSTERBERG. I am.

MICHAEL. Should we practise?

OSTERBERG *tickles the tip of his own nose.*

NANCY. And then we stand?

MICHAEL. In unison. Yes.

OSTERBERG. You grab your coats and follow me.

MICHAEL. Don't scratch your nose by accident, will you?

NANCY. You gonna speak?

TERRY. He's got to say, 'See you in court.'

OSTERBERG. I'll do the signal. I say, 'See you in court.' And then we go. (*Beat.*)

NANCY. What happens if they don't come running after?

OSTERBERG. It always works. You strike a deal right beside the elevator.

The door creaks open slowly so he stops. They stare at it for a moment, wondering if anyone will enter.

Cautiously, a MAN *pops his head round the door. He is fresh-faced, bespectacled, dressed in his shirtsleeves and bearing a tray of coffee. Like an eager young intern.*

When he speaks he is overwhelmingly charming and utterly personable.

MAN. I'm sorry.

OSTERBERG. Can we help?

MAN. I brought coffee. (*Puts it down.*)

OSTERBERG. Ah. Two sugars. I'll get her.

He exits.

MAN. Wow. Can I just shake your hand? (*Shakes* MICHAEL*'s hand.*) Here in person! The giant-killers.

MICHAEL. 'Giant-killers'?

MAN. What they call you. In this office.

MICHAEL. Do they? Oh…

MAN (*affects a cockney accent*). 'I've come about a position. House parlourmaid.'

He grins. Beat. No one knows how to respond.

Don't tell me you don't get it.

MICHAEL. Er... Well... No...

MAN (*Scottish accent*). 'We have reason to believe you stole a chicken from the larder.' (*Still they are confused. Tries his cockney accent again.*) 'Get on with your scrubbing, girl.' Honestly? English people really don't watch *Upstairs Downstairs*?

MICHAEL, TERRY *and* NANCY (*realising*). Aah.

MAN. Most popular show on TV. You knocked it off the top spot.

MICHAEL. Oh. I get you. 'Giant-killers'!

MAN. I loved you in that sketch: 'Nudge Nudge'.

MICHAEL. That's Eric Idle.

TERRY. We're in a meeting, man.

MAN. Of course. I'll just lay these out. (*In silence, he starts to lay out coffee cups.*) Would be great if they put back the cuts.

Silence. Everyone is surprised.

The Indian slave boy. Made me die.

MICHAEL. Oh. You saw it?

MAN (*nods. A half-whisper*). This meeting – all the censorship. It sucks, yeah? Can't be too funny with a gun to your head. I'm a writer. (*Finishes laying out cups and shakes their hands.*)

MICHAEL. Working here?

MAN. Uh-huh. In this department. It's always so frustrating. Everyone meddling. I mean, imagine if art was made like this. Huh? Everyone with a brush, doodling over your painting.

MICHAEL. Er...

MAN. Michelangelo paints the Sistine Chapel and the Pope says, 'Lend me your stuff. I want to add a little section.'

MICHAEL. Er...

MAN. Imagine Rodin delivering his masterpiece – then ten executives all turn up with chisels. How's it going?

MICHAEL. What?

MAN. Progress. The deal.

NANCY. Well...

MAN. You got a list? The things you want restored?

NANCY. Well, yes. We...

MAN. How many?

Beat. They are surprised by his foresight.

You're not expecting them to give way on everything?

NANCY. You think that would be unrealistic?

MAN. No. Just...

MICHAEL. What?

MAN Just... (*A long beat.*) egotistical.

Pause. They stare. Totally wrong-footed.

TERRY. 'Egotistical'?

MAN. Mm. Yeah. Expecting them to broadcast your stuff – with no edits at all.

MICHAEL. 'Egotistical'?

MAN. Uh-huh. You imagine. If anyone could say what they liked. In front of millions of viewers.

The MAN *starts to help himself to the coffee – a change of status.*

What if anyone could walk in with a video – wham it straight in for transmission. With no kind of discussion.

Silence. Everyone is surprised by this.

That's why ABC has done this, isn't it? Protecting you. From self-indulgence.

Beat.

MICHAEL. You're Howard Myers, aren't you?

Pause. MYERS *smiles and drinks.*

MYERS (*sweet and charming*). I wrote a letter – my first month. I wrote a letter to another network. I was angry. I wrote something truly defamatory. My secretary – Sheila. She typed all my letters – she typed that one. (*Drinks.*) Of course, she read it as she was typing – she could tell I was angry. She could see the letter was risky.

NANCY. She censored it?

MYERS. Saved my career.

TERRY. You think Sheila should get your job? We're okay with that if you are.

Breath. MYERS *laughs.*

MYERS. She offered a second opinion. That's all. One glance. A second pair of eyes. Is any of us really so accomplished that we can't learn from someone else, from time to time? (*Beat. Smile never fades.*) You're not used to the process, I know. But frankly you've been lucky. Wrapped in a blanket at Wood Lane. What happens at the BBC these days? They just hand you the keys to the studio and walk away?

NANCY. Mr Myers…?

MYERS. Just imagine it – a TV station that didn't have to go begging to the commercial sector. 'Here's a million bucks of taxpayer money. Go and make a few TV shows. And we promise not to meddle.'

NANCY. Mr Myers…?

MYERS. It must be like a picnic, every day – public cash up front, no public scrutiny. We're answerable to money, I'm afraid. We won't just bankroll your programme.

MICHAEL (*portentous*). Not without conditions.

MYERS (*a gentle laugh*). You come from a different culture. You've been lucky. You've been spoiled...

TERRY. Oh, well then, thank God you're here...

MYERS. Some precocious kid – he's starting out school – he's feels he's got a lot to say. Two schools of parenting, aren't there? How do you deal with this kid?

MICHAEL. 'Kid'?

MYERS. Squash him? Teach him to conform? How to make it through the day? Or do you give him a very big pulpit – thirty minutes on the BBC. Every Thursday. (*Breath.*) It's liberal parenting – the BBC. Soft, liberal parenting. Take all your writers and radicals... give them thirteen episodes of prime time and let them get all their anger out of their system. I'm working in a different system. People don't get paid here for having the loudest voice. We don't give out a fifty-grand budget and a slot in the schedule for being the sassy kid in the class! You want us to broadcast your show – it needs popular appeal.

TERRY. No naughty bits.

MYERS. Yes. I suppose.

TERRY. No rough edges.

MYERS. No.

TERRY. No strong flavours. Just fast food. Bland.

MYERS (*soft sadness*). That's what popular culture is, Terry. Clue's in the title – 'popular' – means it doesn't offend the majority of people. I know to you that's not a badge of honour, but in here, I'm afraid, it's everything we covet. (*Beat.*) Now. You need to make a decision. Are you content to be stuck in your little niche market? Or do you want to find a wider audience? (*Taps his finger on the document – the list of cuts from the tape.*) Thirty-two cuts. The price of joining the goldrush.

FRANKLIN *and* OSTERBERG *enter to recommence the meeting.* MYERS *stands.*

Give Miss Franklin your list – the ones you want restored. Your minimum requirement. Let's barter.

TERRY. A 'tit' here and a 'bumhole' there.

MYERS (*laughs*). Yes.

TERRY. We'll advance you two 'tits' for a couple of 'assholes'.

They all laugh.

FRANKLIN. Shall we?

And MYERS *is leaving. Scene fades.*

6. Office

The lights come up on the same conference room.

Two hours have passed. Everyone looks tired and rather dishevelled. All the coffee has been consumed. Pieces of paper have been scribbled on and then thrown around – the table is drowning in documents.

FRANKLIN *is leading the negotiation.*

OSTERBERG *and* NANCY *are on the other side of the table, arguing.*

MICHAEL *is lying with his forehead on the table and his arms stretched out, clutching great handfuls of paper – no longer able to participate.* TERRY *has completely given up on the meeting and is concerned instead with his collage of art, to which he has added plenty of new obscene drawings.*

FRANKLIN. I can't.

OSTERBERG. We must…

FRANKLIN. I can't.

OSTERBERG. We must…

FRANKLIN. I can't go back to them. I can't go back to them with this. It is our industry… standard!

OSTERBERG. We have a baseline. Six separate cuts.

FRANKLIN. I can't go back.

OSTERBERG. We want restored... six.

FRANKLIN. I can't...

OSTERBERG. It's non-negotiable. Sorry.

FRANKLIN. It's not arbitrary. None of the changes here...

OSTERBERG. We must...

FRANKLIN. We have our standards and practices. And we must adhere...

OSTERBERG. Six separate cuts. Without these, the whole style...

FRANKLIN. I can't.

OSTERBERG. It's non-negotiable.

FRANKLIN (*reading*). 'The hot-blooded bisexual navigator.' (*Beat.*) Just explain to me...

TERRY *and* MICHAEL *sigh audibly.*

TERRY. We've done this.

MICHAEL. We've just explained...

FRANKLIN. Please! Explain just once more...

TERRY. It's the whole damned basis for the comedy.

FRANKLIN (*reads from the document again*). 'The tender compassionate story of one man's love for another man in drag.'

OSTERBERG. It has to stay.

FRANKLIN. Because? Because... why?

TERRY. Without it – there isn't any joke.

NANCY. A war film. It's supposed to be a war film.

FRANKLIN. I see.

She doesn't see.

About bisexuals.

TERRY. The point… It juxtaposes them…

FRANKLIN. 'The pilot, Jennifer…'

TERRY. 'And his love…'

FRANKLIN. 'For the bisexual navigator.' (*Breath.*)

MICHAEL (*mutters from his recumbent position*). She's not saying it right.

FRANKLIN. I'm sorry?

MICHAEL. You're not saying it right. You're not.

NANCY. Mike…

MICHAEL. It's supposed to be a voice – a pompous cinema announcer.

TERRY. That's the joke.

FRANKLIN. I see. The voice?

MICHAEL. Like in a war film. (*Looks up. Does the voice.*) 'Coming to this cinema…'

FRANKLIN (*flat, humourless*). 'The secret love of bisexuals.'

MICHAEL (*near the end of his tether*). There's a type… there's this type… British war films. The type of film where all the men are old-fashioned heroes. The announcer describes them in this voice. Their story. Only this time…

FRANKLIN (*unmoved*). He's saying they're bisexual.

MICHAEL. Yes.

FRANKLIN. It doesn't seem all that funny. (*Beat.*) I'm not sure we'd miss it. Not that one little moment.

OSTERBERG. 'The secret love of bisexuals'?

FRANKLIN. I'm not sure we need it.

MICHAEL (*under his breath*). I'm not sure either, to be honest.

FRANKLIN. Let's move on, then. The slave boy.

MICHAEL *and* TERRY *sigh again*.

NANCY. We've already said…

FRANKLIN. Please. Just let me see if I understand this correctly. (*Breath*.) Two women are watching the TV, and every show they watch is a repeat.

NANCY. We've been over this.

OSTERBERG. Twice already.

FRANKLIN (*ignoring her*). One of them – she reaches over and presses a button – a button with a cable attached – and… at the other end of the cable… there's this little Asian slave boy, standing naked in a loincloth.

NANCY. Look…

FRANKLIN (*speaking over her*). And when the woman presses the button the current flows into his nipples and gives him a shock. (*Beat. Looks up*.) Can somebody tell me, please what's funny about that? Shocking a boy in a turban?

MICHAEL (*looks up. Strong, assertive*). Nothing.

FRANKLIN. What?

MICHAEL. It's not actually funny.

FRANKLIN. You're agreeing with me.

MICHAEL. Yep. I never realised until now.

NANCY. Mike?

MICHAEL. Having heard you describe it, then – I think it's lousy.

NANCY. Mike. Hang on…

MICHAEL. Not one single ounce of comedy.

FRANKLIN (*a gentle smile*). We can lose it, can we?

MICHAEL. Why not?

FRANKLIN. 'The slave boy'?

OSTERBERG (*quietly, to* NANCY). That was on our list of six.

NANCY. Mike, shall we take a break here?

    MICHAEL *struggles to his feet. He's had enough.*

MICHAEL. Lose them all! The dancing Queen Victorias.
Special gaiters...

TERRY. Mike...

FRANKLIN. You really think...?

MICHAEL. Mm. Let's just have dead air!

    *He is tearing up a page from the document – wilder and
wilder. Finally his temper surfacing.*

After hearing your bold new reading of the scripts from
series four, I'm beginning to regret writing any of it. Ditch
the whole show! Just broadcast a slogan: 'Sorry, Michael
Palin isn't funny. We've only just realised.'

FRANKLIN. Mr Palin...

MICHAEL. Nothing – NOTHING – is going to seem funny if
you dissect it under a microscope. We're talking about the
one true spontaneous expression – laughter – and you're
asking for a recipe.

NANCY. Mike, stop...

MICHAEL (*to* OSTERBERG). Please – I'm begging you to do
it.

OSTERBERG. Er...

MICHAEL. Or I will.

OSTERBERG. The thing?

MICHAEL. Uh-huh.

OSTERBERG. You want me to...?

MICHAEL. What was it?

OSTERBERG. Went like this.

    OSTERBERG *tickles his nose with his finger.*

NANCY. Was that for real?

OSTERBERG *nods. They all stand.* FRANKLIN *is suddenly confused.*

FRANKLIN. What's going on?

TERRY. An historic moment. First time in thirty years Michael Palin throws a fit.

MICHAEL *stuffs the paper confetti in his fist and puts it to his lips. He blows it across the table with an enormous raspberry. The paper pieces scatter.*

Beat. The rest of them watch him in silence – TERRY with a wide smile of admiration. And then they rise in unison.

OSTERBERG. We're getting nowhere.

NANCY. So we're leaving.

FRANKLIN (*suddenly panicked*). Look, I have... I have to broker a solution...

OSTERBERG. Doesn't seem to be happening. Thank you for your time, Miss Franklin.

NANCY. Don't forget to say it.

TERRY. Loud and proud.

OSTERBERG. We'll see you in court.

TERRY *punches the air.* OSTERBERG *grabs the two videotapes and shoves them into his briefcase, clicking it shut. The Pythons head out of the door and the scene spills out into the open-plan office.*

FRANKLIN *pursues them, with a wad of disorganised notes in her hand.*

FRANKLIN. We've given ground.

NANCY. Not at all.

FRANKLIN (*reads her notes*). 'Special gaiters.'

OSTERBERG. You've given one. We wanted six. Please just press the button, Nancy.

FRANKLIN. And in the Hamlet sketch. 'Legs up on the mantelpiece.' We made headway.

OSTERBERG. Did we?

NANCY. No.

FRANKLIN. We did. You kept it.

NANCY. No. We kept half.

FRANKLIN (*checks her notes*). Two times you get to say it. 'Legs up on the mantelpiece.'

OSTERBERG. Four times it's in the script.

NANCY. Four separate references to sex.

FRANKLIN. We cut half. You keep half. Feels fair to me.

MICHAEL (*finally he shouts*). Not to me it doesn't. No. It feels like congenital insanity! You hate it. It offends you. I get that. But your brilliant solution – you'll allow us to get away with half! Would Michelangelo's *David* look sweeter if you left one bollock peeping out and covered up the other?

FRANKLIN. Mr Palin...

MICHAEL. 'Sorry, Titian, the brushwork is fab, but we're slightly worried that both of her breasts are in the frame.

FRANKLIN. I... Look...

MICHAEL. Maybe if you add a vase or something. One nipple's fine but two – it feels like overkill. Lose it, can we?'

They pile into the waiting elevator and OSTERBERG *holds the door open.* MICHAEL *is at the front of the group railing at* FRANKLIN.

Sound of an elevator door pinging incessantly whilst it is held open.

OSTERBERG (*trying to negotiate*). Maybe if we...

MICHAEL. I'm a carpenter. That's my job. Okay? What you're destroying is a crafted show that I made. It may not be entirely to your taste but don't bring along a hacksaw when you appraise it!

OSTERBERG. Right. Maybe if we...

MICHAEL. You don't buy a Chippendale table and then whine because the bloody thing is half an inch shorter than you'd like! Don't buy it! Buy another bloody table! But don't sit there and tell the maker how to reconstruct it!

OSTERBERG (*trying to talk over* MICHAEL). Last chance...

MICHAEL. What is it about TV commissioners? You're the only bloody patrons of the arts who carry on this way. You resent us for doing it alone. You think nothing really good can be happening without your signature.

NANCY. Mike, let Robert say...

MICHAEL. You don't look at a piece of art and think, 'What is this? What does it say to me? How does it speak?' You fucking look at it and start to imagine, 'What can I turn this into with a bit of a tweak?'

OSTERBERG. If you'll allow me...

MICHAEL. Go and find another one, will you? Find another picture you can mess up. I like mine as it is. I can't sit through another five minutes of 'you got half and we got half'. (*To* NANCY.) Hit the button.

NANCY. Mike...

MICHAEL. Fucking hell! I'll do it.

And he does. The sound of the pinging door ends abruptly. The door closes and we hear the elevator descend. FRANKLIN *is left up on the twenty-first floor.*

Soft tinkly music plays. There is a long long silence before anyone can speak.

I'm sorry everyone. She niggled me.

TERRY (*dry, amused*). It was pretty tough to get a feeling on that, Mike. (*Breath.*) Mike was niggled in the meeting, everybody. Did you happen to notice?

NANCY. Okay. We have to go back up there.

OSTERBERG. And say what? 'We'd like to be friends now.'
Hold hands in a circle. (*Breath.*) They're gonna need suits,
Nancy.

MICHAEL. Why?

OSTERBERG. 'Cause you're in court tomorrow morning.

NANCY (*genuinely shocked*). You said that was never gonna
happen!

TERRY (*still amused*). Mike got niggled and he blew it.

MICHAEL (*composed*). I couldn't sit there and pretend. They
are saying there is one voice allowed. One song America can
sing. (*To* OSTERBERG.) I *want* that fight. Federal court.
Tomorrow morning. I want to stand up and throw a punch.

TERRY (*smiles*). Arthur Pewty. You're a man.

The elevator arrives at the bottom floor and the doors open.

End of Act One.

ACT TWO

7. Zoo

Opening music: Simon and Garfunkel – 'At the Zoo'.

MICHAEL *and* TERRY *loitering, done up warmly for the winter weather. They stamp their feet to keep out the cold.*

MICHAEL *has a styrofoam cup of coffee.* TERRY *has a balloon in the shape of a tiger.*

MICHAEL *is nervous, irritable.* TERRY *is in fine form – looking forward to his day.*

MICHAEL. *You* get the head.

TERRY. What?

MICHAEL. *You* get the head.

TERRY. What do you get? If I get the head.

MICHAEL. I get the rest. (*Breath.*) I mean the body. The tail. And the body. I'll have the end with the tail...

TERRY. If it's an issue.

MICHAEL. Yes. It is.

Pause. MICHAEL *drinks.*

TERRY. Empty.

MICHAEL. What?

TERRY. This place.

MICHAEL. December. A day in the wild kind of loses its appeal. Where d'you get the balloon?

TERRY. On the sidewalk. Sorry. Did you want one?

MICHAEL. Nope.

TERRY. Nice-looking wildebeest.

MICHAEL. I'm fine.

Pause. MICHAEL *stamps his feet because he's cold.*

Do you *have* to say 'sidewalk'? (*Breath.*)

TERRY. As opposed to what?

MICHAEL. There's a perfectly good word!

TERRY (*smiles*). You feeling the pressure?

MICHAEL. It's like you're trying to be… challenging.

TERRY. To who?

MICHAEL. Whom! (*Mutters, almost to himself.*) Throw words up in the air like you're shuffling cards. (*American pronunciation.*) 'Leisure.' 'Herb' without an 'h'. 'Buoy!' That's the one that really makes my skin crawl. 'Buoy.' (*Beat.*) Hey – yesterday I heard this girl talking. She said, 'Don't touch my shit.' I sat there thinking, 'Who the hell would want to?' (*Pause.*) 'Basil.' 'Oregano.' 'Pyth*on*.' 'Hey! Which one of you guys is actually Mr Pyth*on*?'

TERRY (*American pronunciation*). 'Buoy' is right.

MICHAEL. No, it isn't.

TERRY. 'Booo-eeey.' It's an accurate rendering of the vowels.

MICHAEL. Don't pretend you love America. You left.

TERRY. I didn't leave because of how they pronounce the word 'buoy'.

Silence. TERRY *thinks about the word for a moment – and then tries it out.*

Booo-eeey. (*Pause.*) Booo-eeey. What do you guys say?

MICHAEL. Boy.

TERRY. Really?

MICHAEL. Yep. Simple. No frills.

Silence.

TERRY. Booo-eeey. (*Pause.*) Booo-eeey. (*Pause.*) Come to think of it, it does sort of get up your ass a bit.

NANCY *appears in her winter coat.*

NANCY. Everyone ready?

MICHAEL. He gets the head.

NANCY. Okay.

MICHAEL. And I get the body.

NANCY. You might wanna rethink the plan.

MICHAEL. Is there a problem?

NANCY. Well, the head is the easy bit.

MICHAEL. Really?

NANCY. It's a python. The body's over sixteen feet long.

MICHAEL. The body can't bite you though, can it?

TERRY. It can give you one hell of a hug.

MICHAEL. Shit. I hadn't thought. Is there a part that isn't dangerous to hold? Maybe we could stand outside the cage and just point.

NANCY. Oh, sure. The press would love that. I'm trying to get something memorable – something iconic.

MICHAEL (*to* NANCY). It would look a whole lot better than a shot of me shitting my pants whilst I'm constricted by a snake.

NANCY (*looks at her watch*). Well, let's not stand here and argue. We're due in court in half an hour. Let's give 'em something they're gonna wanna print.

TERRY. Michael's death would probably tick the box. (*Offers his balloon to* MICHAEL.) Hold this. I need a crap.

And he exits. Silence.

NANCY. Thanks for this.

He doesn't respond.

I know how you feel. (*Breath.*) Courting the press...

MICHAEL (*irritable*). If you're telling me it's what we've got
to do...

Pause. Nothing to say.

NANCY. For the film I did a thing.

MICHAEL. Film?

NANCY. Last year. 'And now for something...' Your movie.
The New York debut. (*Beat.*) Isn't easy – getting attention.
Everyone told me: British humour wouldn't catch on.
Sometimes you have to dick around.

MICHAEL. What *did* you do?

NANCY. I just pogoed up and down outside the theatre. (*Beat.*)
In a Girl Scout uniform. (*Smiles at the memory.*)

He doesn't smile.

MICHAEL. I don't understand. You're smart. You're a capable
person. Why would a job like this attract you? Bellowing at
people just to get their attention?

NANCY (*shrugs*). Helps if you believe in what you're selling.

He looks at her.

I was a fan before I worked for you. (*Breath.*) Spent my
career touting rock bands round radio stations. Pretending
they're the next big thing in music. Most of it, you know,
was shit. But – hey – you think about the grocery bill and try
to fall in love with it. Gotta tell you, it was one hell of a
relief when they asked me to do promotion work for you. If
you're trying to make the folks come to Jesus – kinda helps
if you're rooting for him too.

*Beat. She is staring at him, thinking how to phrase her next
question.*

MICHAEL. What?

NANCY. You okay about today?

MICHAEL (*incredulous*). 'Okay'?

*Beat. She reaches into her pocket and produces a scrap of
paper, gives it to him.*

NANCY. Your wife called.

MICHAEL (*perusing the message, smiles*). Asking what to get the boys for Christmas.

NANCY (*treading carefully*). It doesn't say that. It doesn't say 'What should I get?'

MICHAEL (*looks sharply*). It's not your business.

NANCY. Sorry. I couldn't help but read it. (*Pause.*) You know what happens? If you lose this thing? The hearing; the injunction. If the decision goes against you. (*Beat.*) Have you thought about damages? Court costs? They're gonna try and crush you. They don't want a queue forming behind you.

MICHAEL (*bursts*). For God's sake, Nancy! You came to me!

NANCY. Yes.

MICHAEL. A week ago. You stood there in my garden. 'Michael, get on a plane.'

NANCY. I didn't think that it would get this far.

MICHAEL. You didn't think I'd lose my temper.

NANCY. Actually, I was told you didn't have one.

MICHAEL. No. You asked me because I'm the quiet one. I wouldn't fuck up your publicity campaign.

NANCY. I just thought…

MICHAEL. Uh-huh. You thought you'd get a story.

NANCY. You weren't supposed to walk out.

MICHAEL. I wasn't supposed to give a toss, you mean! I'm so sorry that my moral outrage got in the way of your media event. Of course, it never occurred to me you didn't give a damn about the show – you just wanted a headline.

Pause.

NANCY (*smiles*). You don't like me. (*Beat.*) It's okay. I understand.

MICHAEL. Why are you trying to persuade me to back out *now*?

NANCY. Because it doesn't say, 'What should I get them?' *I* took the message. It says, 'What can we *afford* to buy?'

Silence.

MICHAEL. Okay. What's the alternative?

NANCY. Settle.

MICHAEL. Mm, I think the mad hippy might have something to say about it.

NANCY. Terry doesn't have a wife back at home with a stack of bills in one hand and a letter to Santa in the other. (*Rather shamefaced.*) I've got what I need.

MICHAEL (*with no joy*). Yes, of course.

NANCY. You got on a plane. You came over. I've already got the headline. Phone their lawyers. I'll set it up.

MICHAEL. Look...

NANCY. I don't want to be responsible for turning your life upside down.

Pause.

MICHAEL (*turns to her*). I can't, sorry. I have to keep going. 'You're too vulgar; too extreme. You're not welcome in America.' (*Looks at the note from his wife.*) He wants a fort. He said. Soldiers. A fort. (*Gentle irony.*) Maybe he'll settle instead for his dad being brave.

Scene fades.

'The Liberty Bell' is heard in its original form as it did on the TV shows – a rousing brass band. It accompanies the men as they dress for court and file into the room...

8. Courtroom

A simplistic interpretation of the courtroom.

JUDGE MAURICE LASKER *presiding on the bench in the middle.*

There are two tables – one on either side – and with the bench they form three sides of a square. The audience is the fourth side.

At one table sits OSTERBERG. NANCY, MICHAEL *and* TERRY, *the plaintiffs, enter and join him.* OSTERBERG *has placed the two videotapes in front of them.*

At the other table is CLARENCE FRIED, *the trial lawyer for ABC. He is joined by* MYERS *and* FRANKLIN.

A chair in the middle of the square represents the witness box.

8a. Introduction

The march dies away.

LASKER *begins his opening speech.*

LASKER *is dry and intelligent but oddly casual in his delivery.*

LASKER. I get unhappy. You can see it right here. (*Pointing to himself.*) This is my unhappy face I'm wearing today. Two groups – from the media industry – two groups of people have proceeded in good faith. (*Points to* TERRY *and* MICHAEL.) These men sold their TV show, unaware that it was about to be changed. (*Points to* MYERS *and* FRANKLIN.) The network decided to create an edited version. Standard practice in US television. (*Breath.*) No

one's tried to deceive the other. No one has wilfully
committed any crime. Yet here we are, in a federal court.
Ready to do battle. Me with my unhappy face. Go figure.
(*Consults his papers. Reads them out more formally.*) I'm
here to rule on a request for an injunction, submitted by the
plaintiffs – Messers Palin and Gilliam. The injunction relates
to their TV show – due for broadcast on the network. They
want it off the air. (*Looks up.*) I got to say it's unusual, fellas
– trying to get your show taken off the biggest network in
America. I read today that we're all making history.
(*Glances at his watch.*) Right, we've got eight hours.
Someone's gonna leave here with a frown.

He looks over to the plaintiffs.

Mr Osterberg? Shall we get stuck in?

OSTERBERG. Your Honour?

LASKER. You want to go ahead and start arguing the motion?

OSTERBERG. I'd prefer to make an opening statement.

LASKER. You favour the conventional route?

OSTERBERG. I do.

LASKER (*sighs*). Pity. Well. Go on, then.

   LASKER *leans back in his chair and gestures for*
   OSTERBERG *to begin.*

OSTERBERG. My clients – Terry Gilliam and Michael Palin –
   they're employed as scriptwriters at the BBC. Their show –
   it was commissioned by the BBC, filmed, then edited and
   broadcast in the autumn last year. (*Holds a document in his
   hand.*) I have here their writers' agreement – a copy of which
   I have given to Your Honour.

LASKER (*waves it*). I thank you.

OSTERBERG. Section five states: after they've submitted it…
   no one has the right to make changes to the script. (*Beat.*) No
   one has the right to make changes.

LASKER (*slightly surprised*). I heard you the first time.

OSTERBERG. I was just repeating it. For emphasis.

LASKER. Okey dokey. 'No one has the right to change it.'

OSTERBERG. Not without the writers' full consent. (*Breath.*) ABC have given a statement conceding that *this is indeed* the case.

LASKER. I hardly think that they concede, Mr Osterberg. Or why are we sitting here?

OSTERBERG. They say so. In their affidavit.

OSTERBERG *reaches for a second document and holds it up.*

'ABC does not have the right to change a single word of the script.' Sworn statement.

LASKER *looks at the defendant's lawyer,* FRIED, *but he does not stand to object.*

LASKER. Okay. This might be quicker than I thought. (*Mutters.*) Shame. 'Cause I ironed my shirt. And the gown's just been laundered. (*Sits back in his chair and ponders.*) Okay. Okay, okay, okay. I presume this is all just an honest mistake.

OSTERBERG. Your Honour?

LASKER. When ABC bought the show… they *thought* they'd bought the right to change it.

OSTERBERG. And they hadn't.

LASKER. Exactly. So… Wadda ya say we ditch this? We have a cup of coffee. Settle this like friends.

OSTERBERG. Your Honour…?

LASKER. What about waffles? Everyone likes waffles. Big sugar rush and we'll cheer up and get the thing settled. (*Silence.*) Tell me, why are we all so eager to spend the next eight hours in litigation? I liked my waffles with banana. How 'bout you guys? (*Silence.*) No? Well, sometimes worth a try. Okay. Who's your first witness?

'The Liberty Bell' march swells again.

*It fades in and out between each section of Scene 8,
conducting the protagonists from one scene to the next as if
they are part of a marching band. Thus the whole of Scene 8
has a pompous, majestic feel as a result of the music.*

8b. Nancy Lewis Direct

NANCY *takes the stand.*

OSTERBERG *is questioning her under oath. She's nervous.*

NANCY. A big part of the BBC empire is 'BBC Enterprises'.

OSTERBERG. And their function is what?

NANCY. To exploit all BBC programmes.

OSTERBERG. 'Exploit'?

NANCY. Yes. With books; records; even T-shirts.

OSTERBERG. I see. Yes.

NANCY. 'Enterprises' sold the show to ABC in June.

OSTERBERG. And when was it broadcast?

NANCY. October. Four months later.

OSTERBERG. What was your reaction to the broadcast?

NANCY. We were disappointed.

OSTERBERG. How… disappointed?

NANCY. Because of the editing.

OSTERBERG. What did you do?

NANCY. I got in touch with ABC. By cable. I asked to see a
tape.

OSTERBERG. And they sent one?

NANCY. Eventually. I had to call them up first.

OSTERBERG. And what did you do with the tape?

NANCY. I took it to London.

OSTERBERG. Why?

NANCY. To show the writers. There's a clause in their agreement – no editing without their full consent.

FRIED. I must object.

LASKER. Ah. Mr Fried, hello – I was beginning to worry about you, I confess.

FRIED. This clause is in no way relevant.

LASKER. You concede that it's true, in your written affidavit. I thought that was rather reckless of you – I thought it might come back to bite you in the leg.

FRIED. We agree that it's true, Your Honour. We are simply saying that in this situation it's not relevant.

OSTERBERG. It's a binding agreement not to edit. My clients have complete script approval.

FRIED. Exactly. Yes. (*Breath, for effect.*) This contract specifies: no changes can be made to the *scripts*.

LASKER. What you got?

FRIED. My clients didn't change the scripts – they changed the video. A totally separate entity.

Pause. It sinks in.

OSTERBERG. Your Honour…

FRIED. We fully concede, Your Honour, the plaintiffs have the final word on *scripting*. It's just a shame that when they wrote this they never thought to mention 'celluloid' too.

Pause.

LASKER. Mr Osterberg? Sounds good to me.

OSTERBERG. Your Honour…

FRIED (*reads*). 'Scripts must not be altered prior to filming.' They weren't. They were filmed as agreed. What happened after that isn't covered in this document.

OSTERBERG. Your Honour, this is crucial to our case. Clear breach of copyright.

LASKER (*shakes his head*). Mr Fried is right. It may be crucial to some cases – but not this one. What else you got in that big fat file on your desk?

Pause. OSTERBERG *struggles hard not to look crestfallen.* MICHAEL *hangs his head.*

OSTERBERG. Miss Lewis. Will people think less of your clients – after this TV programme has been aired?

FRIED. I must object.

LASKER. Well, you're on your feet already.

FRIED. This is pure speculation.

LASKER. Yes. Of course it is.

FRIED. You're asking the witness to guess what will happen after Monday night's broadcast? Shall we also seek her opinion on what the weather will be doing tomorrow afternoon?

LASKER. Mr Fried – we are here to establish if this programme will be damaging at all. We can't do that without *some* speculation. So let's lay off the grumpy sarcasm. (*Breath.*) Miss Lewis?

NANCY. This edited version – the 'essence' has been lost.

LASKER. Can you give us a little more help?

NANCY. My clients are 'cutting edge' comedians. This version… it makes them like Jack Benny.

LASKER. I like Jack Benny.

NANCY (*back-pedalling suddenly*). I'm saying it's been turned into something it wasn't.

LASKER. 'If they want Jack Benny they should have hired him.'

FRIED. Your Honour, Jack Benny is actually the client of my client.

LASKER. Well, I'd give you extra points for that – if only I could.

A sudden turnaround – OSTERBERG sits and FRIED stands – this is now the cross-examination. We move from one to the other seamlessly.

FRIED. Miss Lewis, do you work in New York?

NANCY. I have an office at Seventh and 53rd.

FRIED. So you're only one block away from the ABC tower?

NANCY. Yes.

FRIED. And did you ever walk over? Did you ever knock on their door and ask to see the tape?

NANCY. No.

FRIED. No. You sent a telex. And then phoned. After the broadcast?

NANCY. Yes.

FRIED. Despite your close proximity.

OSTERBERG. Your Honour, she has already answered the question.

FRIED. You learned about the sale of the series in June this year. The sale to ABC.

NANCY. That is so.

FRIED. But you didn't ask for an edit until after it had been broadcast, four months later?

OSTERBERG. Your Honour…

LASKER. Mr Osterberg!

Beat. NANCY is uncomfortable.

NANCY. No.

FRIED. Would it be fair to say you were… sluggish?

NANCY. Mr Myers – he was reluctant to return my call.

FRIED. I have your telex, requesting the tape in *October*.

NANCY. It wasn't just me. There was some delay from their side.

FRIED. 'Some delay'?

NANCY. I sent them a telex. They didn't respond so that's when I tried to call.

FRIED. We've three days to go until the next broadcast. Who's responsible for running out the clock?

LASKER. Just hold on. (*Beat.*) I thought we all proceeded in good faith. Suddenly I find the facts are in dispute...

FRIED. Your Honour...

LASKER. It's a miscommunication, surely. Not a filibuster. Or am I just floating off on my own little happy cloud? (*Beat. Looks at them.*) If Miss Lewis is saying that the tape was withheld, then that's a whole other story.

Beat.

FRIED. Miss Lewis?

NANCY. They were *slow* to respond.

FRIED. Not as slow as you were to make the request in the first place.

Beat.

LASKER. Miss Lewis? Are you saying they were... obstructive? (*Breath.*)

NANCY. No.

FRIED. No. The delay was simply your mismanagement. (*Beat.*) You waited till October to ask. That's how much your clients' reputation means to them.

Silence. NANCY does not know what to say. She looks over at TERRY and MICHAEL – apologetic.

'The Liberty Bell' plays again as NANCY marches away from the stand and MICHAEL approaches. They pass one another in the empty space.

As the scene wears on the musical phrases become more broken and tuneless.

8c. Michael Palin Direct

MICHAEL*'s turn on the stand.* OSTERBERG *has a copy of a script in his hand.*

OSTERBERG. How are these scripts put together?

> MICHAEL *opens his mouth to speak and is immediately interrupted.*

FRIED. You Honour…

LASKER. Ah. Mr Fried. Hello. You stretching your legs again?

FRIED. The scripts are not the issue.

OSTERBERG. I wish to demonstrate a willingness to submit to sensible editing.

> *Beat.* LASKER *nods.*

> (*To* MICHAEL.) Please.

MICHAEL (*deep breath*). The meetings are tough. We all shout.

LASKER. You shout?

MICHAEL. The scripts are read out. We argue. Some are rejected. Good scripts go into a pile.

OSTERBERG. So… you edit each other?

MICHAEL. Yes. There are actually six of us. We write in different teams. I write with Terry Jones. There's… rivalry in the room. It's a very harsh environment. Sometimes we get up and we fight.

LASKER. Doesn't sound very sensible.

MICHAEL. Maybe it's not. It can be reckless and angry but it *is* always democratic. The scripts are something we agree on. Maybe that's why we're defending them so vociferously. It's like… it's like a chemical compound. Made up of these six different elements. You remove any one of these things – the compound doesn't work in quite the same way any longer.

OSTERBERG *takes a breath. New tactic.*

OSTERBERG. What's been the effect of these cuts?

MICHAEL. Well, the work has suffered.

OSTERBERG. And will this affect your reputation?

FRIED *stands up.*

LASKER. Mr Fried, I see you. I'll allow. Maybe try to stay in your chair occasionally. (*Breath.*)

MICHAEL. Yes. This version makes no sense. With phrases taken out.

LASKER. Can you give us an example?

OSTERBERG *hands* MICHAEL *a copy of the script. He thumbs through it to find an example.*

MICHAEL. Well... there's the army sequence. From the Entertainment War. The sketch is about a court martial. The counsel is trying to examine a deserter on the stand. And the Judge keeps interrupting.

LASKER (*deadpan*). Why's that funny?

MICHAEL (*to* LASKER). Well. The Judge keeps on stopping him and asking him questions about the tiniest details.

LASKER. Like what?

MICHAEL. The counsel mentions Basingstoke and the Judge wants to know directions for how to get there.

LASKER. Basingstoke?

MICHAEL. Yes, Your Honour. In England.

LASKER. How *do* you get there?

Beat. No one laughs.

Sorry. I was trying to be amusing.

MICHAEL (*gesturing to the script*). Perhaps if... perhaps if I were allowed...

LASKER. You wanna give us a taste?

MICHAEL. Would you mind?

LASKER. Sure. You need Mr Gilliam?

TERRY *gets up and goes over to the stand. He has a second copy of the script – flips to the same page.*

FRIED. Your Honour, do we have time for a whole performance?

LASKER. Mr Palin is trying to illustrate his point so I can understand exactly how it's changed. We can read the edited version after.

FRIED. Your Honour, I respectfully suggest that it wouldn't be as funny.

LASKER. That's what we're trying to establish.

FRIED. I mean, if you've already heard the sketch. The jokes will not be fresh. The plaintiffs have an unfair advantage.

Beat. LASKER *sits back and considers.*

LASKER. You think because I've heard *their* version all my laughter will be spent before I get to yours.

FRIED. Your Honour…

LASKER. Unless you want to rewrite the federal law, the plaintiff always gets to bat first.

FRIED. Yes. But, Your Honour…

LASKER. I love to laugh, Mr Fried. How I love to laugh. I've got laughter in my soul for you both. Let's hear it.

Music.

8d. Recess

MICHAEL *drinks coffee and eats a sandwich on a park bench. A street band is playing Christmas carols in the background.*

OSTERBERG *strolls over. They both wear their winter coats.* MICHAEL *is cheerful and upbeat about the morning.* OSTERBERG *doesn't smile.*

MICHAEL. Didn't laugh.

OSTERBERG. No.

MICHAEL. Not a titter. Not second time around. Not a sausage.

OSTERBERG. I saw. I heard.

MICHAEL. Chuckled his nuts off first time. Listened to the edit in stone-cold silence. Huzzah. I never thought I'd be so delighted that a sketch of mine was really badly received. Praise be – we totally tanked! That'll be a hundred thousand dollars, please.

OSTERBERG *sits.*

You're not smiling. (*Beat.*) I mean – you're not smiling... even *more* than usual. He thought the cuts were bad! He has a copy of the Lanham Act somewhere.

OSTERBERG. Yeah. He does. But he's also got a pocket calendar.

MICHAEL*'s smile fades fast.*

No one's gonna convince this guy that you've come here for the sake of your reputation. (*Breath.*) Four months she waited...

MICHAEL. You're not blaming this on Nancy...

OSTERBERG. She works two damned streets from where the tapes were being edited! (*Sighs.*) I told you, you had to have an answer. I warned you – think of an answer. First time we met. She wastes time, pushing you in front of cameras. You should have been preparing. This is how they're gonna beat you!

Silence.

MICHAEL *eats.*

MICHAEL. None of us are very 'business-smart'.

OSTERBERG. You think I haven't worked that out for myself? I'm one of the best media lawyers in this city. I've represented scores of other professionals. First time I've ever had a client that forgot to turn up for the meeting. (*Shakes his head.*) Seventy-five days! If I win this it's going to be my finest hour. I'll go to Lombardi's and order a big steak. With your name on it.

Beat. MICHAEL *laughs a little to himself.*

MICHAEL. 'Professionals.'

OSTERBERG. What?

MICHAEL. Sounds – a bit odd. When you call us that.

OSTERBERG (*dry*). I'm using it in its broadest possible sense.

MICHAEL. We're not professionals, we're schoolboys really – cracking smutty jokes; scrawling them on the desktops. Getting our own TV show – it wasn't like someone handing you a career. Half-hour at eleven-thirty. It was more like being patted on the head and given sweets. (*Eats.*) Success, just… crept up on us all. We didn't see how big it was gonna be. No one takes you aside at the start and says, 'Get yourself a lawyer.' You're too busy finding your way.

OSTERBERG. You need to speak to your management. Get her reassigned.

MICHAEL. 'Sacked.' You mean 'sacked'.

OSTERBERG. Yes. I do.

MICHAEL. Well, then say so. Don't invent a new word. Not when there's a perfectly good one. (*Beat.*) What is it about you people?

OSTERBERG. Lawyers?

MICHAEL. Americans. American *lawyers* worst of all. You think solving a problem just means finding who's to blame. And then it's all wrapped up in a bow.

OSTERBERG. Two hundred million Americans. Know how many of them have got TVs now, do you? It's the biggest pulpit in the world. You can't leave it in the hands of kids. They can't run the show. (*Points over his shoulder.*) Two years ago – exact same courtroom that we're in today – they arraigned John Mitchell. Watergate. Two hundred million Americans. Nine out of ten saw the thing on TV. That's what killed them. (*Breath.*) Just 'cause the girl hangs out with rock stars, doesn't mean she's qualified to represent *you*. You're not a student pulling faces. Not any more. You're in a position of power. You need people to take care of you.

Beat. OSTERBERG *stands.*

MICHAEL (*sighs*). Know many people, do you, who would pogo up and down in fancy dress to get attention? She's been loyal.

OSTERBERG. Then buy her a carriage clock and send her on her way.

MICHAEL (*shakes his head, depressed*). God. This country makes me want to vomit.

OSTERBERG (*half-smile*). I guess in Britain no one complains if their coffee is cold.

MICHAEL. Yes, and people have the right to fail.

OSTERBERG (*shrugs, facetious*). 'You say potato.'

MICHAEL. That's the right pronunciation.

OSTERBERG. You're back on the stand in five minutes. Cross-examination.

OSTERBERG *goes. The music plays and the protagonists march back into court.*

8e. Michael Palin Cross-examination

MICHAEL *on the stand*. FRIED *cross-examining*.

FRIED (*reading from a script*). 'Naughty bits.'

MICHAEL. Yes.

FRIED. Two words. Removed. (*Reads*.) 'So on June 7th 1783, the Montgolfier brothers had a really good wash. Starting with his face and arms, Joseph Michael Montgolfier went on to wash his torso, his legs and his… er, naughty bits.' (*Pause. Looks at* MICHAEL.) Why's it funny?

MICHAEL. Er, well…

FRIED. You submit that without these two words the show is not as funny?

MICHAEL. Yes. I do.

FRIED. Why's it funny?

OSTERBERG. Your Honour, where's this headed?

FRIED. I am trying to establish what has been lost in the edit.

LASKER *nods for* OSTERBERG *to sit*.

It's a genital reference?

MICHAEL. Yes.

FRIED. 'Naughty bits.' His penis and his testicles.

TERRY *bursts out laughing suddenly*. MICHAEL *smiles, points at* TERRY.

MICHAEL. Indeed.

FRIED. Why not just say 'penis and testicles'?

MICHAEL (*shrugs*). It doesn't sound as silly.

TERRY. Until a lawyer says it.

LASKER (*a reprimand*). Mr Gilliam. Please.

Beat.

FRIED. How funny is it?

OSTERBERG. Your Honour...

FRIED. Two words, extricated from ninety minutes of film. If the writers think these words are so significant, I wish to establish the precise extent of the damage.

Again LASKER *nods for* OSTERBERG *to sit.*

How funny?

MICHAEL. There's no measure.

FRIED. Some may laugh. Others will be stony-faced.

MICHAEL. Yes. Yes. I expect so.

FRIED. So. The show will be diminished in the eyes of *some*. But not others. Not all. When the words are removed. (*From his notes.*) Absurdity, allusion, analogy, exaggeration, faulty reasoning, play on words, reproach. Freud tells us in his writing that there are only seven types of joke. (*Beat.*) Which is this?

MICHAEL. I... I really don't know.

FRIED. Is it clever humour? Wordplay?

MICHAEL. No. Of course not. No.

FRIED. Would Noël Coward use it?

TERRY *really has to stifle his laughter this time.*

MICHAEL. You seriously asking?

FRIED. Would Coward use the words 'naughty bits' to make a joke?

MICHAEL. It's not Coward. This is... schoolboy humour.

FRIED. Some will laugh. Some won't. But the people laughing will be 'boys'?

MICHAEL. Look...

FRIED. This will play in a late-night slot. How many boys do you think will tune in at that time?

OSTERBERG. Your Honour...

LASKER *shakes his head.*

FRIED. The impact will only be lessened for people who appreciate smutty childish humour.

MICHAEL. There's not an age limit on what we do!

FRIED. You just said...

MICHAEL (*bursts with frustration*). Laughter's unpredictable. That's what makes it so enjoyable. It's a random event. A burst of energy. Something we didn't even know we had inside. You can't put people into teams and say, 'You're not gonna laugh 'cause your balls have dropped. Stick with *Private Lives*!' (*Breath.*)

Everyone a little surprised by the strength of the response.

Children love clowning, yes of course. They love 'silly'. Naughty humour. But it's not their exclusive domain. There's a child hidden somewhere in most of us, still desperate to laugh. We're trying to make him come alive.

FRIED. Why?

Beat. MICHAEL *nonplussed.*

MICHAEL. 'Why'?

FRIED. Why is it necessary to reduce an adult viewer to the level of a child? (*Breath.*)

MICHAEL. 'Why be silly?'

FRIED. You're an educated man. (*Refers to notes.*) Four years at Shrewsbury. Three years at Oxford University. Why devote yourself to infantile humour?

MICHAEL *ponders for a moment. And then...*

MICHAEL. I'd like to answer that question in two ways, if I may. (*Breath.*) Firstly in my normal voice. And then in a kind of squeaky high-pitched whine.

Beat. And then the tension breaks – LASKER *laughs. Others too.*

See. Four hours of cross-examination. One silly joke can completely change the mood. That's the power of it. It's life-affirming. Sometimes you have to blow a raspberry at the world.

Music.

8f. Lee Franklin Direct

FRANKLIN *on the stand.* FRIED *is questioning.*

FRIED. How much, Miss Franklin? Exactly.

FRANKLIN. It's hard to put a figure on.

LASKER. Maybe you could estimate.

FRANKLIN. Eighty thousand, in advertising revenue.

LASKER. You'd lose all the advertisers, if you lost the show?

FRANKLIN. I think, many. (*Breath.*) Fifty-six for the show itself.

FRIED. Thousand? Fifty-six thousand?

FRANKLIN. Yes. And fifty-six thousand to replace it.

LASKER. So we're saying… a hundred and ninety?

FRANKLIN. Yes.

LASKER. What you'd lose today, if I grant the injunction?

FRANKLIN. I think. (*Breath.*) There's also 'reputation'. Hard to put a figure on.

FRIED. Whose reputation?

FRANKLIN. The network. We have a bond with the viewing public. This show has been advertised in the press for weeks.

FRIED. And if you made a substitution – your reputation with the public would be… tarnished?

FRANKLIN. Twenty million people tune in. They feel some sort of bond with us. We're like… an old friend.

FRIED. What would happen if the show was broadcast with no cuts at all?

FRANKLIN. That too would be damaging.

FRIED. Why?

Beat. She considers.

FRANKLIN. There is a sketch in the programme where an Indian slave boy is tortured with electrodes.

FRIED. And you've cut it?

FRANKLIN. We've cut it because… well, racial tolerance is a key issue here today. I don't doubt that in Britain this is harmless, but in the US we have significant social problems.

TERRY *tuts quite audibly.* FRANKLIN *turns to him a fraction.*

These men are from a different era – a different social background, certainly. Privileged. Untouched by racial violence. Untouched by reality. In their privileged world – it's still funny to take out your anger by beating a slave; or by zapping him with electricity. Still funny to imagine a woman with her legs up on the mantelpiece during intercourse.

LASKER. But surely – they're not promoting these things. They're not promoting racial violence, are they?

FRANKLIN. They are pointing a finger that way. And they're laughing at it. That's a big concern, I should say. (*Breath.*) There's a kind of blanket assumption – artist: good – network: out of touch. But we're not the ones responsible for depicting every women under thirty as a feather-brained blonde. We're not the ones responsible for dressing up a man in a loincloth and a turban and then giving an electric shock to him to try and raise a laugh. It depends what you consider to be funny.

8g. Howard Myers Cross-examination

MYERS *on the stand.*

MYERS. There are two kinds of cuts that are necessary –
irritating, yes, but necessary all the same. First there is the
mechanical kind – the kind that we use to fit something into
our schedules.

OSTERBERG. You're talking about ad breaks?

MYERS. Yes. We had to cut twenty-two minutes to fit with our
format. Like it or not, we're a business. Commercials pay the
bills. (*Pointing to the videotape on the table.*) They gave us
the money to buy that. (*Breath.*) Secondly... there are the
cuts that will make a show conform to our standards and
practices charter. Censorship.

OSTERBERG. And that's a legal requirement?

MYERS. Yes. It's fundamental. Basically, our hands are tied
there.

OSTERBERG *pauses for effect.*

OSTERBERG. It's quite a coincidence.

MYERS. I'm sorry?

OSTERBERG. That the two should... tally, so precisely. You
remove things to satisfy the law. And the space is exactly
long enough to give you your ad breaks. (*Breath.*) Do they
usually coincide?

MYERS. No.

OSTERBERG. No. So. What do you do if they don't? How to
proceed? (*Breath.*)

No response.

You've satisfied the law. Say – you're still five minutes short
for the ad breaks. What's the next stage? (*Breath.*)

MYERS (*with some reluctance*). We use our discretion.

OSTERBERG (*seizing on this slip*). Aah! You 'use your discretion'. To make up the shortfall.

MYERS. Yes.

OSTERBERG. So now you're saying there are three types of cuts? (*Numbering on his fingers.*) Standards, ad breaks and now there's your personal opinion.

LASKER. Mr Osterberg?

OSTERBERG. I'm saying, Your Honour, that in this matter there are no hard-and-fast rules. Mr Myers has stated that these cuts are not based on his opinion. Clearly, that isn't so. (*Breath.*) Taste is a factor.

MYERS. Yes. Okay.

OSTERBERG. You edit for... merit?

MYERS. Sometimes. Yes. We do. (*Breath.*) I thought the shows were frankly 'poor'. Not funny. Not a patch on any of their previous work.

OSTERBERG. The BBC had shown them intact.

MYERS. And they'd axed the series – after only six episodes! One ingredient was missing.

LASKER. 'Ingredient'?

MYERS. The lead actor. Gone to make a show of his own.

Beat. MICHAEL *and* TERRY *visibly bristle.*

That's why the BBC only commissioned six episodes. Instead of the usual thirteen. The sketches didn't work without him. I felt that some judicious cutting would help.

OSTERBERG. One actor can't have made that much difference...

MYERS. Americans actually believe that Monty is one man. The tall one in the bowler hat. John Cleese. Your clients – they're simply not as funny now he's gone. They pretend that they're here with a noble cause; they can toss around a word like 'reputation'. Truth is – they can see their careers all slipping away from them fast, and they're angry about it.

Music plays.

8h. Second Recess

MICHAEL, TERRY, NANCY, OSTERBERG *storming out of court*. TERRY *apoplectic*.

TERRY. Fucking shit.

NANCY. Hey.

TERRY. Fucking arrogant bastard. I'm jealous! I'm jealous of John. That's why I've come! Somebody put a rifle in my hand.

MICHAEL (*pushing him away*). Terry, for God's sake, keep your voice down!

NANCY (*to* OSTERBERG). What happens now? Which way's it gonna go?

OSTERBERG. Too close to call.

TERRY. Fucking arrogant dickwad.

OSTERBERG. They won on copyright. *And* on reputation.

NANCY. And that stuff about John…

OSTERBERG (*nods*). Throws doubt on your motivation. (*Beat.*) All we've got left is…

MICHAEL. Lanham.

OSTERBERG. That's our case. The show is a pale imitation.

MICHAEL. Okay.

NANCY. Will that do?

OSTERBERG. Wouldn't stake my reputation on it. (*To* TERRY, *very severe*.) Hey, keep it under control. Or don't come back in the room.

And he sweeps off with NANCY.

Silence. TERRY, MICHAEL *alone. No one knows quite what to say.*

And then…

TERRY. Fucking shit.

MICHAEL. He was right.

TERRY. What?

MICHAEL. Myers. That's why you're so angry right now. That's why it feels… raw.

TERRY *stares at him.*

It's not as funny. The fourth series stinks. We're guilty for being found out. Doesn't work without John. If we'd painted the *Mona Lisa* – if we'd written Shakespeare – we wouldn't be shouting so loud. Cut a hole in a masterpiece – the desecration speaks for itself. Don't need to start a row. (*Beat.*) We turn up and start bartering for jokes – bloody obvious there weren't enough there at the start. Myers was right. We're finished. And we're angry. Whatever other shit he's come out with – today he hit the mark.

Breath. Clasps TERRY'*s shoulders.*

TERRY *breathes deeply, smiles.*

Music plays. They trudge back in for the verdict.

8i. Verdict

LASKER *gives his verdict from the bench.*

LASKER. Time is of the essence – I know that both parties are anxious for judgement right away. (*Reads a prepared statement.*) I find that both sides in this dispute today have acted entirely in good faith. (*Breath.*) The plaintiffs sincerely hold the view that their work should be shown as they created it. They are justified in seeking to defend that right by bringing it to federal court today. I believe that American Broadcasting tried to edit to serve the public interest. They were aware of the… sensitivity of some of the material – and so removed it. (*Beat.*) So far so good. Everyone is knocking on my door with the best of intentions. So… I am left to decide what damage – if any – this version may cause if shown. I find that the plaintiffs have established *some* impairment in the integrity of their work. It fails to deliver the… iconoclastic verve. It is simply a pale imitation, in fact. (*Pause.*) It's a very heavy cut. It certainly comes near the borderline of, let's say… the point at which a wound – though not fatal – will make it hard for the patient to live in health. Nevertheless, there are reasons why I *cannot* grant the injunction as requested today. The ABC network *will be allowed* to broadcast their edited version on Monday.

Pause.

The room freezes over.

First there is some serious question as to who owns the copyright on the material. The BBC has been… lackadaisical in failing to provide a representative here. I cannot rule for breach of copyright without them here to clarify the terms of the sale. (*Beat.*) The network has demonstrated it will suffer financial loss if the injunction proceeds. Under those circumstances there has been a disturbing… casualness from the plaintiffs. Seventy-five days have elapsed between the first broadcast and the court date. This gives ABC precious little time to find a replacement, and that has financial implications. The plaintiff's motion for a preliminary injunction is hereby denied.

He bangs his gavel. The protagonists start to chatter.
MYERS *and* FRANKLIN *are ebullient.* MICHAEL,
TERRY *and* NANCY *are all utterly crestfallen.*

TERRY *takes off his tie in disgust and throws it on to the table.*

But... (*Breath.*) I am willing to consider a motion for more limited relief.

Pause. They all look at him, waiting.

Mr Osterberg, I must tell you I have in mind a second possibility – some kind of statement to be written and attached to the front of the show. A disavowal. 'The writers hereby disown what follows.' You know... Something of that kind. It will affirm that the show was completely re-edited, without your clients' full consent.

OSTERBERG. Er... When can we make this motion?

LASKER. In the next two minutes?

MICHAEL. Oh, fine. As long as we're not rushed.

OSTERBERG. Your Honour...?

LASKER. You gentlemen must sit down now and agree on the actual wording that you want. Then you can run it past me for judgement first thing Monday.

FRIED. But, Your Honour...

LASKER. And I'm telling you, Mr Fried. I'm likely to agree. The network will still have time to film it and add it to the front of the show that goes out in the evening.

He bangs the gavel again and the court rises.

'The Liberty Bell' march swells again. Scene fades.

9. Hotel

MICHAEL *and* TERRY, *exhausted.* MICHAEL *lies on the bed – * TERRY *on the floor.*

MICHAEL *has a wet flannel over his face.* TERRY *has a piece of paper on his chest and a pencil between his teeth – he is composing something.*

For a long time neither can speak.

MICHAEL. What's the choice again?

TERRY. Asshole.

MICHAEL. Or?

TERRY (*checks his paper*). Turd. Turd or asshole.

MICHAEL. Depends a lot on what we're trying to say. (*Breath.*)

TERRY. We're trying to say we hold him in the deepest contempt. Turd or asshole?

MICHAEL (*thinks*). I think either one covers it, frankly.

Beat.

TERRY. Turd one. Asshole two.

MICHAEL. That's how I would go.

TERRY. And what about a prefix?

MICHAEL. How d'you mean?

TERRY. What kind of turd? Let's specify. (*Beat. Thinks.*) Fucking turd.

MICHAEL. Total turd.

TERRY. Smelly turd.

MICHAEL. We're drifting into the realms of what my kids might write. (*Beat*.) To be honest, we've gone past the point where they're gonna let us put the thing on telly. It's supposed to be a disavowal.

TERRY. Yeah.

MICHAEL. 'The writers want to distance themselves from what you're going to watch.' We start calling Howard Myers a 'fucking turd', I think we could be risking a whole new legal challenge.

TERRY. 'Turd' is definitely your favourite, is it?

MICHAEL. Things you hoped you'd never hear someone say to you.

Silence. They stare at the ceiling.

TERRY. What's next?

MICHAEL (*suspicious*). How d'you mean, 'next'?

TERRY. We write this – we stick it on the front of the show. What then?

MICHAEL. Then I go home and burn my fucking passport.

TERRY. Really? You don't want to fight on?

MICHAEL. God no. Never again.

Pause.

TERRY. What about an appeal?

MICHAEL. On what grounds? You're insane. And tenacious. And frankly you expected to win? Old Saint George is the Patron Saint of 'I've-had-enough-I'm-going-back-home-to-get-the-beers-in'.

Pause.

TERRY. This is gonna be the last gasp, Mike.

MICHAEL. What?

TERRY. The BBC – the one we know and love.

MICHAEL. What's it got to do with them?

TERRY. Guys like Myers – they're gonna get hold of it; shake it up; demand results; make us justify every cent. The producers that we grew up with, the ones who placed a value on what we do, they'll be pensioned off, put out to pasture. Corporate America will come marching down Wood Lane, I betcha. (*Beat*.) The BBC, it's my life raft. You know?

MICHAEL. I do.

TERRY. I go down to that sound-effects place in White City, and I play there, I make little tapes, I'm like a kid with... a jigsaw, I soundtrack all the cartoons. They all know me, there's no expectation, there's no one breathing down your neck to get a result. There's something... academic about it, just fill the place with people see what develops.

TERRY finally staggers to his feet.

Gotta fight on. It's not just me being me. I'm not just yelling for the sake of yelling. Not this time. England is the only place that listens. It's the whole future of television. We have to appeal against this verdict.

TERRY slopes off to his adjoining room to pack.

Pause. MICHAEL staggers to his feet. He starts to pack his things. His suitcase was never found so he has barely anything to pack – just the few items of clothing that NANCY bought him.

There is a knock at the door. He goes to answer. It's NANCY.

NANCY. You alone?

MICHAEL. I'm packing. What little I have.

She rushes in and shuts the door – speaking quietly, almost conspiratorially.

NANCY. Got to talk to you.

MICHAEL. I know what you're going to say. (*Wanders back to his packing*.) Not quite the result we were hoping for. They fuck up our show and they take us to the cleaners too. Hooray.

NANCY (*confused*). 'Take us to the cleaners'?

MICHAEL. It's a phrase. It means… Oh, bollocks. I'm not bothering to stand here and translate. 'Arse-about-face.' 'Bee's knees.' 'Bob's your uncle'. Why did we think we could ever make it big in the States? Making jokes about the Liberal Party! And chartered accountants!! The English sense of humour stops at Dover.

NANCY (*interrupts his tirade*). Myers called me up!

Beat. MICHAEL *stops dead and stares at her.*

He wants to see you. (*Breath.*) Just you.

MICHAEL. Why not Terry?

NANCY (*shrugs: 'Dunno'*). The man probably values his testicles.

Beat. He considers.

MICHAEL. He wants to make peace then.

NANCY. Go and see.

MICHAEL (*and then he realises*). He wants to stop us shooting our mouths off in the press.

NANCY. There's a chance… there's a chance he might consider…

MICHAEL. Oh, I get it. If I grovel…

NANCY. The damages…

MICHAEL. You think he'll waive them?

Beat.

NANCY. Come on, it's the sensible solution. I'm sorry. I really didn't plan for it to end up this way. He's got all the cards. He's beaten us – we're in the dust. At least…

MICHAEL.…if I kiss his bum I won't end up in penury.

Silence. He is deciding.

And then he realises.

You were waiting. Outside. Until Terry went. You stood outside. And listened. And waited. Till he'd gone.

NANCY (*quiet, so* TERRY *cannot hear*). Terry won't agree…

MICHAEL. You're right. He won't.

NANCY.…to play along.

MICHAEL. No. No, he has bigger concerns. Not to mention bloody principles. Whereas I…

NANCY. Mike…

MICHAEL.…I'm just so pliable. You're looking for someone to go along and make peace. Let's go ask Mike – he can mutter apologies. He's so English. He won't embarrass us. He'll always roll over and beg.

NANCY (*suddenly forceful*). You've got to go. (*Breath. Quieter now.*) I have to make you go. That's gonna my last job as your US promoter.

Beat.

MICHAEL. You're leaving.

NANCY. I fumbled the ball.

MICHAEL. Well. As of today that makes you an honorary English person.

He picks up his coat.

Scene fades.

10. Office

MICHAEL *at ABC with* FRANKLIN *and* MYERS.

FRANKLIN. We could work on it together. Your statement.

MICHAEL. Together?

FRANKLIN. We could do something… 'jokey'.

MICHAEL. Ah. Right. I see. (*Beat.*) One last chance to aim a blow. And you want to soften it. Right. I follow your reasoning. (*Breath.*) A disavowal. But 'jokey'.

FRANKLIN. Mr Palin…

MICHAEL. Just another gag. Make it look like we don't really
care.

FRANKLIN. Your position…

MICHAEL. Yes.

FRANKLIN.…today, having lost the case. Let's talk about
these damages…

MICHAEL. Sure. And then let's talk about blackmail.

Beat. FRANKLIN *looks at* MYERS, *inviting him to speak.*

MYERS. We get to show the edited version. Seems rather
churlish to make you suffer more. We're happy to forego all
the costs.

MICHAEL. If we turn the disavowal into a joke. Is that really
all?

FRANKLIN *pulls out a sheet of paper and lays it on the
desk. Silence.* MICHAEL *reads.*

She offers him a pen so he can sign the document.

FRANKLIN. There'll be no more challenges.

MICHAEL. Ah.

FRANKLIN. You agree to let the Judge's decision rest.

MICHAEL. No more mess in the appeal court.

FRANKLIN. Exactly. You can sign for your colleagues. Sign
there on behalf of all six.

Silence.

MICHAEL. And what if they don't agree?

FRANKLIN. Mr Palin – the bill you face for costs could be
huge. Are you willing to shoulder that burden, simply
because your friend is too tenacious to let go?

Long pause. MICHAEL *stares at the page, and then at*
MYERS.

MYERS. You think I'm the villain here.

MICHAEL. Well...

MYERS. You think I've made it my life's work to confound you? I'm a writer – same as you. A TV writer. I came here to make great shows, not to wag my finger at you.

MICHAEL. Well, then why...?

MYERS. You just don't get it. England – you don't see yourselves. Funny little hotchpotch island. No identity. No values. You've made dissent into the national language. Anyone can say what they want in front of millions of viewers. Television is the medium of the future, but you let people use it to chip away at anything sacred. America has values that we're willing to defend. You pawned yours. It's actually resentment that you feel when you're with us.

Pause. Is he about to pick up the pen?

MICHAEL. Did you laugh?

MYERS. Laugh? When?

MICHAEL. When you saw it? Our show. The uncut version. Did you laugh? Did you think it was funny?

MYERS. Yes.

MICHAEL. Even laugh at the naughty bits?

MYERS. Yes.

MICHAEL. The boobs and bums. Of course you did. Naughty bits are hilarious.

MYERS. Yes, I laughed. I laughed at the naughty bits.

MICHAEL. Good.

A shared smile. But then MICHAEL*'s smile suddenly hardens.*

But you won't let other people laugh, too. Your job is actually rationing people's laughter. No one else is allowed to get quite as much as you.

MICHAEL *stands.* FRANKLIN *stands too – tries to offer him the pen again.*

What's *that* for?

FRANKLIN (*laughs, thinks this is a joke*). To sign.

MICHAEL. Oh, I'm not signing. We're still going to trash the show, when it's out on Monday.

Beat. FRANKLIN *is confused.*

MYERS. I don't follow. Then why did you come here?

MICHAEL (*to* MYERS). To tell you you're an arsehole and a turd. And Terry Gilliam says 'hi'.

And he sweeps out.

Scene fades.

11. Subway

MICHAEL *on the subway. He's fumbling for change.*

A voice makes him turn.

It is LASKER, *wrapped up in his coat and scarf – on his way back from court.*

LASKER. Er… You got a problem there?

MICHAEL. Oh, hello.

LASKER. I've just finished court. Usually travel on the subway.

Beat. They are momentarily lost for words.

MICHAEL. I don't have change. I don't have any money. Which is bloody symbolic, really. After everything that's happened today.

LASKER. You want I should lend you some?

He rummages in his pocket and counts out some money.

MICHAEL. Is this okay?

LASKER. I don't think fifty cents will constitute massive corruption. (*Gives it to* MICHAEL.) You guys flying home?

MICHAEL. Tomorrow morning.

LASKER. And are you coming back again? To appeal.

MICHAEL. Ah. You as well. (*Referring to the money.*) Thanks.

    MICHAEL *is leaving. And then...*

LASKER. I didn't get a chance to tell you, but I loved the PBS shows. I thought Arthur Pewtey was a gem.

    MICHAEL *turns back.*

    And 'Nudge Nudge'. Had me rolling around.

MICHAEL. That wasn't me...

LASKER. No, I know. Eric Idle. Will you tell him?

    MICHAEL, *surprised and delighted.*

    My name's Morris. Morris Lasker. I should say, by the way – my wife. She doesn't call me Morris.

MICHAEL. You make her call you 'Judge' at the dinner table?

LASKER. No – she calls me by my nickname.

MICHAEL. What's your nickname?

LASKER. Monty.

    Beat. They smile and then shake hands.

    I better go.

MICHAEL. What's *your* advice? On the appeal.

LASKER. I'm not allowed to say.

MICHAEL. Oh no.

LASKER. You have people to advise you.

    LASKER *is about to go again. Then realises he has no change left.*

    Oh, dammit. I gave you the last of my money.

MICHAEL. Here. Take it back. Please do.

*Holds it out, but does not give it. It is just hovering there in
the air for a moment. Why?*

MICHAEL *has just had an epiphany – holding the money in
his hand, ready to return it.*

Hang on. They can't make the same case any more.

LASKER. They can't?

MICHAEL. If it goes to appeal. They can't claim loss of
revenue. (*Checks his watch.*) In two days they'll have
banked all the money. They can't use that argument twice.
We could win.

LASKER (*takes the dime back*). Safe flight now.

He smiles and leaves. MICHAEL stands alone.

Freeze.

Spotlight comes up suddenly on OSTERBERG, *reading
aloud from a document.*

OSTERBERG. 'June 30th 1976. Appeal. From the denial of a
preliminary injunction. (*Breath.*) The court orders that
editing of the programme constitutes an infringement of
appellants' copyright. Also mutilation of appellants'
programmes is precluded by the Lanham Act of America.
Judges Lumbard, Hayes and Gurfein presiding. Injunction
overturned. Two hundred thousand dollars awarded to *Monty
Python.*'

The scene moves seamlessly into the next...

12. Garden

Some months later.

A suburban garden – as in Scene 2.

Now it is summer – birds sing and the sun shines brightly.
NANCY *offers the paper to* MICHAEL *and he takes it.*

He reads in silence. After a moment he looks up – gobsmacked.
She smiles.

NANCY. It's alphabetical.

MICHAEL. What?

NANCY. The surnames. 'Gilliam versus ABC.' He starts with a
'G'.

MICHAEL (*shrugs*). Think I'm worried about the billing? It's
the result that matters, Nancy. (*Kisses the page.*) We won at
appeal.

NANCY. They couldn't prove revenue loss. 'Cause the show
had already aired…

MICHAEL.…and they'd banked all the money. Did you
phone? Did you phone all the others?

NANCY (*nods*). Graham, yes. And Eric.

MICHAEL. And?

NANCY. Busy. Filming *Fawlty*. Left a message.

Beat. He reads it again.

Pause. They sit together.

He reads the page again, still not quite believing it. Then
turns and looks at her.

MICHAEL. Thanks for coming. Thanks for bringing this.

NANCY. I wanted to finish the job I started.

MICHAEL. What you doing now?

NANCY. On tour.

MICHAEL. Really?

NANCY. Genesis.

MICHAEL. Cool. Is it cool?

NANCY (*shrugs*). British schoolboys, wanking with synthesisers. (*Beat.*) I heard about *your* 'thing'.

MICHAEL. Ah. The 'thing'.

NANCY. Good reviews. Your first series.

MICHAEL. Yep. Keeps the wolf from the door. And I've been offered a film…

NANCY. Yeah?

MICHAEL. By Terry. He's been banging on about it. Based on a Lewis Carroll. (*Breath.*) I get to play the hero. 'Dennis'.

NANCY. A hero called Dennis?

MICHAEL. Ordinary-bloke-turned-hero. Gave me the script in January. (*Gestures to the document.*) I think our road trip was sort of an audition.

NANCY. It's your time. You've got this 'thing' going on, Mike. This 'everyman' quality.

MICHAEL (*scathing*). That's the 'thing' I've got 'going on'!?

NANCY. Guy next door. You're the guy next door.

MICHAEL (*amused*). Ah. 'Mundane' is my casting.

NANCY. It's a quality that TV adores, pal. America's an open book for you.

MICHAEL. Oh, Nancy, come on – America is over. All that travelling. Besides, first break we get there and we flunk it. We'll only ever be… a cult act now. A student favourite.

Beat. She's staring at him.

NANCY. Those students have grown up now, hon. And some of them work in television.

MICHAEL. What do you mean?

NANCY. I mean, you should wipe off that frown. Two hundred thousand dollars is just the beginning.

MICHAEL. What? What's happened?

NANCY. NBC. I hear they're interested.

MICHAEL. NBC?

NANCY. There *are* other networks, you know. They have this sorta comedy cult show. Ackroyd and Belushi – they grew up watching you. Eric's flying out to do it in October. And I hear on the grapevine they were asking about *you*. They gave a camera to the sixties' generation. They love your stuff, Mike. You're their heroes. Especially after… you know.

An uneasy pause.

MICHAEL. What do you mean, 'Especially after, you know'?

NANCY. The thing with ABC. War with the establishment. It's brought you a whole new raft of fans.

MICHAEL. Your publicity campaign? It actually worked.

Beat. She smiles.

NANCY. Maybe censorship – maybe the court case – was the best damned thing that could have happened here. Seems to me we took a shitty piece of work and used it to turn you into heroes for Liberal America.

Silence. He stares.

MICHAEL (*cold*). And you planned it that way.

NANCY. Mikey, come on…

MICHAEL. Waiting four months. Waiting until the last minute. You knew that they'd cut it. And you knew that we'd saddle up.

NANCY. You're giving me too much credit. I'm a rock chick.

MICHAEL. You sold our crappy last series to the people who'd be most offended. Just for the hype.

NANCY. This is legal history, Mike. Let's not agonise too long about how we did it.

She rummages in her handbag. Inside is a videotape. She offers it to MICHAEL.

MICHAEL. What's this?

NANCY. I've been meaning to show you. It's the second TV special – the one on air in December.

He takes it.

MICHAEL. Did the disclaimer look okay?

NANCY. Er… Not really.

MICHAEL. What d'you mean?

NANCY. They censored it.

He is momentarily shocked. And then he smiles. And then he laughs.

Blackout.

The End.